ACQUIRING SKILL IN SPORT

BOB SHARP

SPORTS DYNAMICS

© 1992

First published in 1992 by

Sports Dynamics

20, Greenway Lane
Cheltenham
GL52 6LB
United Kingdom

4-333 Admiral Street
Woodstock
Ontario N45 5A5
Canada

A catalogue record for this book
is available from the British Library.

ISBN 0 9519543 1 8

Layout and typesetting by Myrene McFee
Cover design by Myrene McFee

Printed and bound by
Selwood Printing Ltd, Burgess Hill

Dedicated to the memory
of my father —
a coach amongst coaches

Preface

Throughout life we never stop learning. The acquisition of information and the learning of a multitude of skills is vital for survival and is central to life's pleasures. In fact, from the moment of birth we acquire knowledge and develop the ability to use this knowledge which helps us deal with daily challenges and also learn new things up to the moment we die.

Of all the things we learn, much is physical in nature, involving bodily movement. Indeed, most of what we know, understand and learn is reflected in physical movement. Even attitudes, feelings and knowledge are expressed through movement, via facial expression, gestures and what we say. Movement clearly plays a critical part in our lives. It has even been speculated that the ultimate role of the brain is to control physical movements!

The variety of human movement and physical activity is also very rich. We all learn a multitude of mundane tasks such as closing doors carefully, tying shoe laces and using knives for cutting, whilst many people extend their skill repertoire to include complicated skills such as playing a musical instrument, driving a car or touch typing. In addition to these activities, many people take part in sport or engage in various types of physical pursuits. Some follow various individual sports such as squash or judo whilst others play team games such as football and volleyball. Aquatic sports, which include diving and synchronised swimming, are also very popular, as are outdoor activities such as skiing, walking and climbing. Some people excel in many different sports and relish the competitive element, whilst others play for recreation or just to be with friends. The variety of activities available and the reasons for involvement are almost endless.

Whatever the sport or emphasis, learning is essentially a three-sided process. The learner who acquires new knowledge and skills is central to this process. A key facet is the environment which surrounds the learner — this would include equipment, facilities, the teacher or coach, advice and help from others, and so on. And there is the actual content of what is learned — the techniques, rules, knowledge, decision making, etc., which defines the sport or activity in question. Each of these three elements is part of a whole and all are inextricably bound together — without one element, the activity would be meaningless and no learning would take place. This book takes a balanced look at all three aspects. The mechanisms underlying the acquisition of skill are described and the conditions under which people learn are examined thoroughly. And throughout, physical activity and sports skills are used as a focus to exemplify and illustrate the key issues.

The strategy adopted within the text is to describe principles and ideas, discuss their merits and weaknesses and demonstrate how they may be applied to good effect in the teaching and coaching of sports skills. Clearly, the reader's background and experience will dictate how much is taken from the book, however, the intention is to change the reader's thinking in one or more of three ways:

1. The book may introduce the reader to ideas and topics which have not been encountered before.
2. It may remind the reader of methods or procedures which have been forgotten and which can be tested and used once again.
3. It may reinforce principles which are currently used. In this sense, the book will confirm what is good or bad practice.

The book will have achieved its overall aim if it makes the reader a better teacher or coach. To do this, the reader will have to take ideas from the book and experiment with them in the practical situation. Books by themselves do not make people better teachers or coaches. Ideas have to be examined and principles used in practice. 'Learning by doing' is one of the first principles of skill acquisition!

Throughout, reference is made to a number of different people who are all concerned with skill learning — coaches, teachers, instructors, and so on. Whilst there is often a clear distinction in the role of these people, the present text attempts to cut across these boundaries and focus on principles which apply to all those involved in helping others to improve their performance. Clearly, not all topics will apply to everyone and many of the ideas expressed are not specific to sport. Indeed, much of what we know about skill acquisition applies also to diverse areas such as creative ability, social learning and the acquisition of language, and common links will be highlighted where appropriate.

The book has been divided into chapters which form reasonably independent sections. The reader does not have to read the entire text to make sense of individual chapters. However, the reader should bear in mind that learning is a complex process influenced by many factors and that a complete picture of skill acquisition can only be understood by recognising the interactive nature of many factors. Cross-references between chapters should help the reader see important links.

The text is written for all students of skill learning — but notably students and teachers involved in physical education/sports studies — and sports coaches. It is written at a level which is broadly equivalent to the National Coaching Foundation's key course programme. In this way, the intention is to present the reader with ideas based on present research and thinking which have currency and practical application. The book is intended as a readable and practical treatise. Readers will not find themselves bogged down with comprehensive detail from scientific documents and esoteric journals. An important addition to each chapter is a list of 'discussion questions'. These are designed to enhance the reader's understanding through the exploration of specific issues and practical situations.

Finally, whilst the book examines issues relevant to an understanding of skill acquisition, it does not take an entirely conventional view on what 'should' be included in a text on skill acquisition. It includes several traditional topics, but also explores a number of others, such as evaluation, skill analysis, 'inner game' coaching and goal-setting which have currency at the present time. Overall, the book is a personal account of those issues which are seen to be of most relevance to students of skill psychology.

Bob Sharp, September 1992

Contents

List of Figures and Tables

Chapter 1

INTRODUCTION

Putting things into perspective

Whilst this book is all about how people acquire skill and how coaches and teachers go about the task of passing on skills to learners, it is worth starting with an examination of how these procedures fit into the overall teaching/coaching process. This is important because it is vital to understand that technical instruction is only one way the coach or teacher makes contact with learners. There is much more to teaching and learning than passing on skills. Sometimes, teachers concentrate on techniques and practice and tend to ignore other, vital things such as whether the learner wants to learn, what are the learner's goals, are they fit enough, are the rules too complex, are techniques appropriate to the stage of learning and so on. Here, it is useful to examine Gleeson's (1984) ideas on the role of the coach. Gleeson identifies a number of issues which are integral to successful coaching. Many of these also apply to teaching. What are they? Gleeson says the coach:

1. Should be a technician. That is, the coach must be able to teach skills — at the right time, in the correct order, at the proper level, etc., and must know what constitutes good technique, how to identify faults and correct errors.
2. Must be a good communicator, be able to inspire confidence through his/her actions, nurture interest and recognise individual differences between learners.
3. Must be a scientist. The good coach takes advantage of knowledge from the various sciences such as exercise physiology and bio-mechanics to help develop not only coaching method, but also the performance of learners. The coach acknowledges the importance of monitoring his/her efforts and those of the learner and of the need to measure progress.
4. Must be a trainer and know how to assess the physical requirements of sport, how athletes/learners should be conditioned and how to plan training programmes over weeks, months and years.
5. Must be a teacher and therefore be able to deal with emotional or moral problems encountered by athletes, establish and engender personal relationships between and with athletes, prepare plans of work, ensure that training is safe and accident free, etc..

Gleeson goes on to explore notions of the coach as an artist, manager, politician, social worker and others. The underlying point being made here is that skill learning is only one facet of a multi-dimensional process. Whilst the teacher's or coach's target may be to improve skill, along the way a number of caps may have to be worn in order to achieve aims. For example, as an analyst the coach will need to understand how skill breakdown occurs. Is it the learner's lack of fitness, poor understanding, lack of confidence or something else? As a social worker the coach will need to examine how he/she organises groups of learners to ensure there are no personality clashes and that groups are equal in their ability, and so on. It is not enough for the teacher to be technically articulate and dwell only on technical issues. Passing on skills to others is all about communication between people. The good teacher is therefore someone who is knowledgeable about his/her sport but who is also sensitive to a whole variety of human needs. We shall explore some of these issues in later chapters.

Theories are good for you!

Most students embarking on a new subject are faced with the problem of trying to learn and understand theories central to their subject. There are many theories about how people learn and one of the difficulties is that sometimes they don't seem to be relevant or make sense. Often they are difficult to comprehend and seem to have little application. How frequently have we heard the cliche 'It's OK in theory, but it rarely works in practice'! It is critical that we clarify these matters at the outset because one aim of this book is for the reader to understand and 'take on board' theoretical knowledge which is applicable to the world of teaching skills.

Let's begin by examining what is a theory through a couple of examples from the sporting world. Suppose two coaches are working with similar-ability gymnasts and that one group learns a lot faster than the other. A third coach who observes this also notes the better group are coached by someone who seems to have a much better relationship with the athletes — takes more time with individuals, offers better advice and is more understanding, etc.. Add to this another situation, this time skiing, and suppose that an aspirant skier is having extreme difficulty progressing beyond, say the snow plough stage. After years of practice she is getting no closer to skiing parallel than when she first began. She then employs a professional instructor who videos her performance and all-of-a-sudden, things improve — she begins to unweight at the correct time, her skis are closer together and her body posture is better. What do these two scenarios suggest? Well, they seem to indicate that feedback information — of a certain kind — is crucial to success. In the first example it is what the coach says and in the second example it is what the learner sees. Suppose we explored this idea and found that it held good in many other situations with different sports and different people. All these observations would lead to some kind of statement/s about the value of feedback in the learning process. For example, it might be concluded that 'long term improvements take place only if the learner receives continuous feedback about his/her performance'. This statement would be a theory or part of a theory about skill learning. A theory is a general statement (or set of such statements) based on observations, experiences and perhaps formal research, which accounts for and summarises numerous observations. Theories are rather like educated guesses which describe or explain how/why things occur. Theories of learning, for example, attempt to explain why people learn, and also describe the conditions which should be met in order for learning to take place. It is important to recognise that theories are tentative. In that they only describe current observations and cannot verify what might hold true in the future, they must always be treated with some suspicion. Indeed, it is just this uncertainty which leads researchers to examine them further. They do this by using the theory to generate or predict other phenomena which they then test. If the predictions hold good then the theory is strengthened (and in time may become a law) but if not, then the theory is weakened and consequently modified or rejected (see Figure 1).

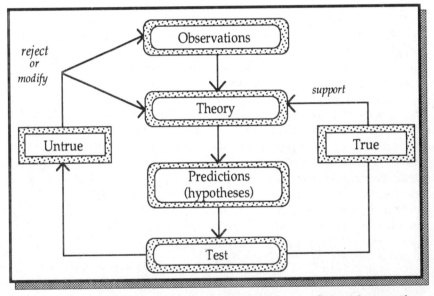

Figure 1:   **The process of testing theories — from observation to theory. Sometimes called the 'hypothetico-deductive method'.**

In the gymnastics example above, it would be possible to make many predictions. For example, if feedback was initially given to a learner — say a gymnast practicing a new floor routine — and then withheld as she continued practice, performance would be expected to increase and then plateau. This could be tested (although it might not be ethical to do it for real — a laboratory equivalent might be constructed) and the results would let us know if the theory was robust or not. Out of interest, the reader may wish to guess the outcome of such an experiment.

Theories, then, are more than single observations, they are generali-sations and they may not always be correct. So what is their value to the practicing teacher or coach? Quite simply, they give direction and structure to ones thinking. They provide a reliable and sound framework within which to work. Rather than trying things out in a piecemeal fashion — 'off the top of your head' — theories allow the teacher and coach to cash in on principles and ideas which have been shown to work or stand a good chance of working. The wise person may have in his/her armour a variety of theoretical ideas and employ underlying principles when they are appropriate and when circumstances demand. This would be called a pragmatic approach. What he or she will find is that theories do not always work nor do they always work consistently. For example, presenting some learners with too much feedback may have the opposite effect to improving their skill level. Effective teaching is therefore the timely application of theoretical principles together with ideas and approaches acquired through experience. In time and with much prac-tice, the good teacher or coach probably develops a personal theory about how people learn best — an internal model constructed from recognised learning theories together with principles derived from effective practice. And of course the good teacher will be prepared to modify ideas and change approaches as experience grows and develops.

It is also worth clarifying at this stage the value of research to the practising coach or teacher. Research provides the 'raw data' for theory construction. Because it is often carried out under meticulous and well-controlled circumstances, there is a tendency to think that research provides clear answers and stable groundplans for action. The view expressed in this book is that research, just like experience and theories, provides nothing more than food for thought and information which the coach can use or discard at his/her will. Magill (1990) is of the view that research can be an invaluable aid to developing teaching guidelines and Whiting (1982: p.12) underlines this point when he says that:

> ... research does not tell people what to do, but only provides some of the information on which judgements might be based as to the value of one procedure rather than another.

Landmarks from the past

The investigation of skill learning goes back many decades and this section takes a cursory look at some of the critical ideas and research landmarks which have led to our present stage of understanding. Sometimes, the ability to understand the present is clearer when it is seen in perspective against historical developments. The past also gives direction for future thinking and ideas for new research.

One of the most often-quoted landmarks is the work of 18th century astronomers at the Greenwich Observatory near London. They noted differences in each other's observations when viewing stars through the telescope. In noting the time of a star's travel some observers consistently underestimated the period of travel compared to others. In addition, these times depended upon how bright was the star and how unexpected its appearance. What the astronomers were actually noting was the difference in reaction time between people. Reaction time is important in some sports especially those where reflex-like actions are required, e.g., sprint starts, goalkeeping.

A century later, Bryan and Harter (1899) carried out what is now recognised as the first formal study of skill acquisition when they examined the manner in which people learn Morse telegraphy (one of the early forms of electrical communication). Morse telegraphy is a complex problem which requires the acquisition of a new language, perceptual skill in identifying transmitted messages as well as motor skill required in sending messages. Bryan and Harter noted two important things. Firstly, that learning is discontinuous in nature. People seem to proceed fairly quickly but then reach a 'plateau' where there is no apparent improvement. After a while they continue to improve once more. Secondly, learners acquire the ability to execute small units of work (e.g., learning how to type single letters) which are later combined into larger units (e.g., typing whole words). We shall examine the validity of so-called plateaus later on. The second point, which has been called 'hierarchical learning', is still very much a current topic and has credibility 90 years after it was first conceived.

During the early part of this century many psychologists set about to examine how and why people learn. Two competing philosophies emerged, namely the Association (stimulus-response or S-R) and Cognitive approaches. We shall come back to these topics later in this chapter, but is important to note here that despite Bryan and Harter's important earlier work, the efforts of the early psychologists did little to further the systematic study of skilled motor performance for the next 30 years. It was during the 1930s that interest in skill learning accelerated through the efforts of researchers in physical education. Investigators, especially in North America, devised practical tests to measure sporting skill and also attempted to identify individual characteristics (human abilities) which predispose people to excellence in sport. During this period, 'time and motion' experts began to look at skill in industrial settings. For example, they assessed how quickly workers carry out tasks (e.g., lathe operations) and what are the factors affecting their speed of working. This work has its modern counterpart in the field of ergonomics. Sports ergonomics is a recent area and is concerned with sports problems such as the design of equipment, the composition of playing surfaces and the manufacture of 'tailor made' running shoes. These matters will be addressed in more detail when we look at guidance in Chapter 3. During the 1940s, research into motor skills accelerated dramatically. The Second World War gave rise to rapid and dramatic technical developments in radar, vehicle control, high speed aircraft, etc., which in turn focused interest on the operational/skill problems this kind of technology presented to the user. The result was an explosion of research — especially by English and North American psychologists — designed to understand the factors which created these difficulties. Investigators looked at problems such as methods of controlling equipment (e.g., use of levers/steering wheels, size of controls), the relationship between displays and controls, and so on (Miller, 1978). Several prominent investigators developed ideas and theories during this time which subsequently spawned a generation of research and which still have currency today. Kenneth Craik, an English psychologist, was the stimulus for the development of many modern ideas. For example, he bought attention to the importance of timing and anticipation in skilled performance and he laid the foundations for the comparison which is often made between man and computers. Frederick Bartlett was another Cambridge psychologist who, based partly on his personal interests in playing cricket, emphasised many important notions of skill acquisition. For example, he viewed feedback as critical to learning and he also believed that complex skills evolved from much simpler skills — a similar notion to that of Bryan and Harter's. Key articles by these and other authors are given in Legge (1970).

The 1950s and 60s saw further advances in research and changes in philosophy. This period saw the development of 'Information-Processing Theory' and with it the view that people and computers communicate and operate in much the same way. The idea that people take in information from the environment, decide what to do about it and then plan and effect a motor program still has some credence and is discussed later. Other people who reached prominence during this time included the American psychologist Paul Fitts who was responsible for, amongst many other things, specifying the stages that people pass through when learning new skills. His three-level theory (cognitive, associative, autonomous stages) was based on comprehensive discussions with teachers, coaches and many others concerned with instructing people. Today, it still stands as a sound description of the learning process. More recently, Jack Adams and Richard Schmidt in North America and David Lees in Scotland have spearheaded research on how people control their movements, focusing on the importance of environmental information and different kinds of feedback in the control/learning process. Notions of motor programming, motor schema and the role of errors in learning, which all stem from their work will be discussed throughout this book. In the 60s and early 70s much attention was given to short term memory of motor skills and comparisons were made between the way in which people remember words, pictures and physical skills. Schmidt (1982) provides a useful historical review. Research on motor memory has diminished in importance in recent years and overall, the emphasis today centres much more on cognitive processes in skill learning (Holding, 1989). Holding's text, which provides in-depth summaries of key areas of skill research, also suggests areas which may be highlighted in forthcoming years. Holding suggests there will be a continuing interest in the deterioration of skilled performance and the related mechanisms of attention and arousal. He also points to the growing development of interactive work between sports academics, kinesiologists, psychologists and physiologists, and to a major trend to align models of skill acquisition with those more commonly used to account for speech production and other cognitive processes.

At present, the field of skill acquisition attracts people from many and varied backgrounds, e.g., physical educationalists, sports coaches, sports scientists, child psychologists, ergonomists, physiologists, and so on. Universities offer courses and employ lecturers in the subject, professional organisations mount conferences and many publications focus on skill learning and skilled performance. In Great Britain, skill psychology is studied at school level as part of the Secondary physical education programme and is a core area in the work of the National Coaching Foundation and the British Institute of Sports Coaches.

The subject of skill acquisition is well-researched and its content and focus continually changes but, unlike the 'hard', human sciences such as anatomy, physiology and kinesiology which benefit from an abundance of concrete, scientific evidence, much of what we know about how and why people learn stems from practical application and educated reasoning. In physiology there are precise and objective techniques for monitoring the inner workings of the body. In contrast, skill psychology has to base its knowledge largely on behavioural evidence and sound reasoning. As Holding (1989: p.291) says, "Theoretical research soon becomes sterile in the absence of the reinvigoration provoked by practical issues." The construction and testing of theories is therefore very much an integral part of this subject. With this as a backcloth, it follows that the present text cannot be a tight, prescriptive treatise which describes neat facts all fitting well together. The intention is to raise issues and provoke discussion, helped with examples from the coaching world, and in so doing lead the reader to think more deeply about how people learn.

We will continue with a brief examination of some of the major theories of learning and skill acquisition.

Staying with tradition

Firstly let us take a look at some of the important findings from early (first part of the century) psychological research on learning. This work was not aimed specifically at motor skills and much was based on animal research. However, many findings are relevant today and are especially appropriate to sport.

Early theories of learning have traditionally been divided into two broad categories: association (stimulus-response) and Cognitive theories. The difference is fundamental and the implications are quite marked.

Association theories

Association or S-R theories consider that learning is dictated largely by the stimuli within the learner's environment and that what is learned is the connection between these stimuli and the learner's movements. Connections are strengthened through repetition and reinforcement of correct S-R associations. Internal processes such as perception, thinking and anticipation have little importance within the S-R scheme of things because they are impossible to quantify in the same way stimuli and responses can be accurately measured. Let us examine some of the important principles of Association Theories.

Conditioning — classical and operant — is the fundamental process of learning. Classical conditioning occurs when a previously established stimulus-response connection is replaced by a new connection in which the response remains the same but the stimulus differs. One experiment often cited is of the dog which salivates (the response) when presented with food (the stimulus). There follows a period when a bell is rung at the same time as the food is presented, after which the dog salivates when hearing the bell alone. In this example, the dog has learned a new relationship — bell-salivation. In humans this kind of learning (sometimes called stimulus generalisation) can occur quite unconsciously, often with negative results. For example, a child who suffers an accident in, say, rugby football, and consequently stops playing, may transfer the dislike to other sports which appear to be dangerous. Positive generalisations may also occur as when someone is rewarded for success in one sport (say, they achieve their first proficiency award in swimming) and then develop newly-found interest in other sports. What is happening in these examples is some kind of transfer — dislike or enthusiasm. This notion of transfer was not accepted by all of the association theorists. Guthrie (1952) viewed that skill comprises a large collection of highly specific associations and that transfering a skill to a new situation only occurs if there has been practice in that situation. Today, we do not accept this very rigid stance, although the principle of skill specificity which was central to Guthrie's theory does have a place in modern thinking as will be examined in a later chapter. We shall also return to the topic of transfer when we look at habit formation and the eradication of errors.

Before leaving the topic of classical conditioning it is important to stress that there are many examples of stimulus-response learning in teaching which are quite appropriate. For example, when trying to encourage a beginner trampolinist to open from a somersault at the correct time the instructor might shout 'Now'. On hearing this command the learner knows when to open and prepares for landing. The learner may not have the experience to 'feel' the correctness of this action, but it does have the desired effect in producing good timing. With further practice, the learner can take over and begin to control the action because she/he learns to associate the internal feelings accompanying the command. At this point the sound becomes redundant. The use of well-timed commands to stimulate action is a very powerful technique and is applied to many sports.

Operant conditioning (Skinner) is quite different and is concerned not with associations between stimuli and responses, but the association between responses and their consequences. Take the sport of artistic gymnastics and the case of a coach teaching an upstart on the high bar. Suppose the learner makes repeated attempts, but is only rewarded positively (e.g., praise from the coach) when the correct/nearly correct technique is employed and that poor attempts are not rewarded. In time, the correct technique predominates, i.e., the upstart occurs more often, because the learner strengthens the link between it and its successful outcome. It follows from this that movements which are reinforced are strengthened, whilst those which are not reinforced are weakened. One of the important features of this theory is that reinforcement must be immediate and certainly occur before the learner has had a further chance to act. A corollary to this theory is the idea of behaviour shaping. Shaping is the process of developing complex forms of behaviour in small steps. In the example just given it was assumed the learner would at some point, actually emit the correct technique. However, this is highly unlikely especially with complicated or dangerous skills. Adopting a shaping regime, the coach would simplify the overall action and reinforce each small step. Through the reinforcement of closer approximations to the correct technique the overall movement is gradually developed. A related idea is that of part learning. One of the S-R psychologists, B.F. Skinner, viewed that difficult tasks must be broken into smaller parts each of which grows out of previous learning. Each part must be reinforced separately and in this way the whole skill is gradually built up. Thorndike was also a sup-porter of operant conditioning and he derived several 'laws of learning' which he believed applied equally well to people and to animals (see, e.g., Thorndike, 1927. Thorndike gave great weight to the outcome of learned movements. He felt that satisfying and gratifying outcomes are more likely to lead to repetition of movements than negative outcomes — hence his 'Law of Effect'. He also emphasised the importance of practice and repetition — the 'Law of Exercise'. Repetition strengthens the association between stimuli and responses whilst lack of practice weakens the asso-ciation. Thorndike pointed out however, that practice alone is not enough — reinforcement must also take place. This idea is still pertinent today and is evident in the statement 'practice, with feedback, makes perfect'. Thorndike's third 'Law of Readiness' was concerned with development of the nervous system and the notion that learning only takes place when the nervous system is sufficiently mature (see Chapter 6).

Cognitive theories

The cognitive or 'Gestalt' learning theories rose to prominence in the 1920s in opposition to the S-R theories. In contrast to S-R theories, cognitive theories attenuate the importance of stimuli and responses and focus on thought processes, the learner's 'mind' and his/her understanding of how things relate to one another. The individual's perception which is determined by a multitude of factors including environmental stimuli as well as internal thoughts, expectations and needs, is the driving force in learning. Understanding, meaningfulness and the individual nature of learning are all critical features.

Some proponents of the Cognitive school of thinking (e.g., Wertheimer, Kohler) viewed insight or intuition as the mechanism of learning. Intuition stems from a problem solving approach. In their experiments with animals they demonstrated that learning is preceded by a period of 'trial and error' learning — although they referred to this period as one of 'purposeful experimentation' — followed by an immediate and permanent improvement. This latter stage was seen as demonstrating the animal's ability to restructure or reorganise all the elements in the display to create an instant solution — the 'Eureka' phenomenon. A good example in gymnastics would be an upstart where the learner who, having already tried unsuccessfully, was then given say an explanation of the mechanics involved and suddenly achieved success — because he/she now understands how actions produce correct technique.

The 'Gestalt' theorists who proposed the notion of insightful learning adhered to the principle of 'whole' learning. Here, learning is not a matter of connecting particular stimuli with associated responses; rather, the learner uses past experience and current knowledge to plan or predict solutions which involve whole and perhaps lengthy patterns of behavior. For the Gestalt theorists, part learning is inefficient because it does not present to the learner all of the information necessary for complete understanding. They would argue that in swimming, for example, the stroke should not be broken down into its constituent parts (arm action, breathing, etc.), but be taught as a whole skill. This idea is consistent with recent emphasis on the "games for understanding" approach to teaching activities. Maynard (1991) for example suggests that teaching/coaching should put an emphasis on the learner making decisions about which tactic should be used in a given situation. He goes on to state that "...most teaching is accomplished by creating conditioning or adapting games rather than perfecting in isolation the techniques required in the definitive version of the activity" (p.11). This philosophy fits in well with the Gestalt approach because it focuses on learner understanding and the 'wholeness' of activities.

One of the Cognitive school, Tolman, put great weight on the notion of goal direction in learning as well as expectation and planning. For Tolman, behaviour was purposeful. Learners consciously strive to achieve particular goals. People learn to recognise cues (e.g., the manner in which a volleyball player prepares for service) and how these cues relate to the solution of specific goals (e.g., how to prepare for and respond to the expected kind of service). Tolman suggested that people acquire cognitive 'maps' or sets of relationships between events — they don't learn movements *per se* — which can be employed on future occasions to solve related problems. Here, he was stressing the importance of past experience in learning as well as the importance of transfer of learning.

Finally, it is important to mention the significance of individual differences within the cognitive theory of learning. Because learning is based on the individual's perception of problems, expectations, motivations and needs then almost by definition people will learn in different ways with varying rates of progress. Lewin (1951) especially stressed the importance of individual traits; the learner's motivations and goals, knowledge and understanding and 'philosophy' of life. Close to this idea is that of 'self-concept'. Self-concept is the individual's perception of himself and is based on a number of things such as the person's physical nature, age, experience, values and needs. By and large, people behave in a way which preserves and/or enhances their self-concept. This suggests that the manner in which they learn and the content of what they wish to learn is dictated by their self-concept. Behaviour, therefore, is ultimately the result of how things 'appear' to the individual. There are important implications here for teaching which include, for example, the need for the teacher/coach to see things 'through the eyes of the learner'. We shall return to this and other issues stemming from the cognitive approach to learning in later chapters. Child (1973) gives a comprehensive summary of traditional learning theories and their applications in teaching whilst Hill (1973) provides a general account of most learning theories.

The two approaches to learning we have summarised are quite different and one wonders how it is that such divergent views on human learning occur. History has shown that people have often 'taken sides', viewing the association and cognitive approaches as mutually exclusive. There are a number of possible reasons. Researchers within each school of thought often set different kinds of tasks — tasks which tended to demonstrate the kind of learning advocated. In addition, experiments were designed largely to lend support for the theory and not to test it. Also, methods of teaching were never a focus of attention. Had they been, then there might have been more of a coming-together of the two approaches. Some authors do not see the two approaches as being independent, but rather as opposite ends of a continuum (e.g., Stallings, 1982). This, more pragmatic view is presently used by many teachers and coaches who employ principles from both schools of thinking which work in practice, as well as ideas from more modern models of learning.

Fitts' theory of skill acquisition

The cognitive and association theorists were not directly interested in motor skill acquisition. Paul Fitts, an American psychologist (Fitts, 1964; Fitts & Posner, 1967) was one of the first people to take a systematic look at skill acquisition *per se*. He based his ideas on laboratory observations of people learning and upon extensive interviews with sports coaches, physical education teachers and instructors in skills other than sporting ones. He asked them questions such as 'What is the most difficult thing for beginners?' and 'How long must a beginner practice before knowing the skill?'. Although there exist weaknesses with his theory, it has stood the test of time and is a very plausible description of the learning process. Fitts reckoned there are three phases involved in the acquisition of skill, although he did recognise that the distinction between them was rather arbitrary.

The early or cognitive phase

The initial stages are concerned with trying to understand what the task or skill is all about. This is a stage where events and cues which demand much attention early on, later go unnoticed. The beginner has difficulty deciding what to attend to and has particular problems in processing information concerning his/her own limbs — hence the aspirant basketball player must watch the ball as it is dribbled and the would-be dancer watches his/her own feet. Early learning is characterised by many and often gross errors and may look like a 'patchwork of old habits' put together into new patterns supplemented by a few new ones. The implications for the coach or teacher at this stage of learning are numerous. Attention must be directed to individual learning styles and methods must reflect the different ways people learn. Demonstrations, instructions and physical guidance are all suitable methods. Cues which are relevant and meaningful to the learner must be selected for emphasis. Practices must be simple but still convey the essence of the sport or skill being learned. Information must be kept to a minimum and potential distractions eliminated.

Fitts used the then-emerging jargon of computer technology (early 60s) and likened the early phase to one where the learner begins to acquire an 'executive program' for an activity.

The intermediate or associative phase

The intermediate phase is so called because it marks a period when old habits previously learned are tried out and are either consolidated if successful or else discarded. Gross errors are gradually eliminated. Actions are better-timed and smoother movement patterns ('sub-routines' to use the jargon again) emerge. The appearance of new movements depends in part on the amount of transfer from previous learning. During this phase, the learner begins to use increasingly more complex or subtle cues and there is an overall change in feedback control from visual/verbal to internal/kinesthetic. It is a period of consolidation of correct or near-correct responses which lasts for varying periods of time depending on the complexity of the skill and the extent to which it calls for new sub-routines and new integrations. A number of key issues concern the coach during this period: the length of practice sessions, the breakdown of complex skills into smaller parts, specificity of feedback, and so on.

Final or autonomous phase

During the final stage of learning, skilled movements become increasingly autonomous, less subject to conscious control by the individual and less subject to interference from other, ongoing activities and environmental distractions. Skills require less processing: i.e., they can be carried out whilst new learning is in progress or while the performer is engaged in other activities. The speed, efficiency and consistency of performance increases, although at a slower rate than previously. Individuals are more able to analyse their own performance and progress does not depend on external feedback or rewards. As far as coaching is concerned, attention can focus on the fine detail of technique or strategy and performers can be encouraged to contribute more and more to their own learning — through self analysis, mental practice and personal motivation.

Modern views on skill acquisition

The last twenty years or so has seen an accelerated interest in skill learning by people from many different disciplines (e.g., see Smyth & Wing, 1984; Stelmach, 1976; Holding, 1989). There seem to be three broad areas which are still the subject of ongoing research and which are relevant to the present text. They are the Closed-loop theory of Adams (1971, 1976), Schmidt's (1975, 1976) Schema theory of skill learning and Information Processing theory,

Adams' closed-loop theory

Adams' ideas on skill learning stemmed from a weakness in S-R theory. He took issue with the notion of reinforcement. In particular, he considered that whilst S-R theories can demonstrate relationships between particular types of reinforcement (e.g., saying "well done") and particular actions (e.g., learning a forward roll), they do not explain why these come about. Adams sought to provide an answer here. In his theory, movements are initiated by what he calls a 'memory trace' and subsequently controlled by another one known as the 'perceptual trace'. The memory trace is developed through experience and based on external knowledge of results about earlier attempts at a movement. Skill learning *per se* involves the acquisition of the perceptual trace which is used as a reference to compare feedback from current movements. The perceptual trace is developed as a result of exposure to various sources of feedback: muscular, auditory, visual, and so on. Through practice, the perceptual trace and feedback are continuously matched. If the match is perfect, the learner proceeds confidently with the movement, but if there is a mismatch the learner's confidence in the correctness of the action is reduced and an attempt is made to eliminate the error. The learning process is one of continuous error nulling throughout the course of making a movement.

Whilst Adams' theory underpins what is undoubtedly an essential ingredient in skill learning, i.e., feedback and knowledge of results, it has a number of weaknesses. One criticism is that for every movement, there is assumed to be a separate memory trace. Given the infinite number of movements which can be performed, this assumption poses a very great burden on the individual's memory capacity. This and other weaknesses are addressed by Schmidt in his schema theory.

Schmidt's schema theory
Like Adams, Schmidt (1975) sought to answer the criticisms of previous theories. He also made an attempt to take the strong parts of existing theories, adding and modifying so as to answer the existing criticisms. Schmidt drew attention to the storage problem of Adams's theory and also the so-called 'novelty' problem. Schmidt reasoned that every movement we execute is different. Even similar movements carried out in the same environment (e.g., a tennis serve) are slightly different in some way. He posed the question that if this is the case, then where does the 'reference' for initiating actions (the 'memory trace' in Adams theory) come from?

To counter this and other problems, Schmidt proposed a 'schema' model of learning. His theory does not rely on fixed memory traces but assumes a generative process developed through experience, feedback and error correction. People store in memory not specific copies of movements for later replication but ideas of relationships (schema) that can be used to produce different but related movements. Each time a movement is performed the individual stores in memory four items:

• The initial state of the muscles and environment prior to a movement.
• A specification of the movement to be produced (forces, speed, timing, etc). This is called a motor program.
• The sensory consequences (feedback) of the movement.
• The outcome of the movement in terms of its success or otherwise in relation to the expected outcome.

Through practice, the learner abstracts relationships between these various sources of information. In time, although the learner forgets the individual movements, he/she remembers the general movement 'rules' (or schema). These can be used on future occasions to predict and implement actions for particular circumstances. In Schmidt's theory, it follows that the strength or utility of schema is directly related to the variability of prior experience. Increasing the amount and variability of the learner's experience leads to the development of increasingly strong schema. This idea has implications of course for the manner in which practice is organised and will be discussed in Chapter 5.

This section has touched on Schmidt's ideas only briefly. More thorough descriptions can be found in Schmidt, (1976, 1982), Smyth & Wing (1984) and Holding (1989).

Information-processing theory
The view of man as a processor of information has been a focus of attention for at least the last 30 years, although the peak of interest now seems to have passed. Information processing theory attempts to explain

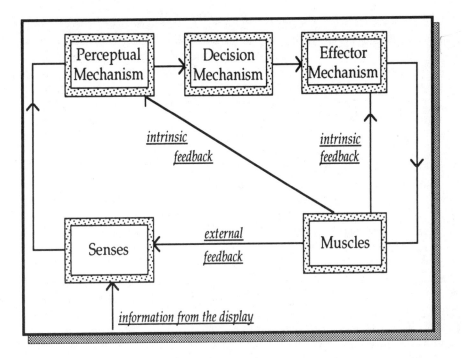

Figure 2: An information-processing model of human performance. Based on Martenuik (1976).

behaviour in terms of stages of central nervous system activity rather
than as a series of actions made towards reaching some goal. Figure 2
shows one particular approach (Martenuik, 1976) from amongst the
many which have been preferred.

In this model there are three major components which process
information between the outside world and actual movement. The
perceptual mechanism which receives information from the display
provides the decision mechanism with a description of the environment.
This mechanism in turn must then decide upon a course of action in
relation to current objectives. Once a particular course of action has been
chosen, a command is sent to the effector mechanism which organises a
response and sends a sequence of signals to the muscular system.

Feedback information is very important and both internal and
external feedback are sent back to several points within the model.
Martenuik's model is typical of most others which differ basically only in
their complexity. Martenuik makes the point that his model could be
further elaborated into a more complicated network of processes and
lines of communication.

The essential rationale in viewing human performance like this is to
break down what is a very complicated problem into manageable

proportions. Researchers are interested in verifying the logic of such models and describing the capacities and limitations of each stage. For the teacher or coach however, the advantages are much more practical. There are at least two particular applications. Firstly, an information processing model provides a logical way of examining the important ingredients comprising skilled action. Describing movements in this way makes sure that nothing important is missed out. For example, before teaching say a snow plough turn to a novice skier, the instructor would assess what are the perceptual, decision making, movement and feedback aspects. He would decide which aspects were relevant and which could be delayed until later. Such an approach would at least guard against an emphasis on technique alone — a common problem in many sports, especially skiing. The second benefit to be gained is related to the first and concerns error identification. Given that learning is largely a matter of solving problems and minimising error there is a need on the part of the teacher or coach to assess the reasons why learners make errors. Through questioning whether the reason is a perceptual, decision making or technical one, the teacher has a systematic and comprehensive tool for eliminating most possible sources.

In many ways, information processing theory likens the individual to a computer or communications system in which information is stored, manipulated, sometimes distorted and finally output. The analogy has also been extended to movements themselves. Here, the overall plan behind a movement has been labeled the 'executive program' and the movements which serve the plan the 'subroutines'. Martenuik gives the example in badminton of an overhead clear (the executive program) which is executed through the action of a number of subroutines responsible for the grip, stance, back swing, forward swing, etc.. Within this framework, learning is a matter of acquiring subroutines which initially take on executive program status, which then become automated with practice. Robb (1972) has extended this idea to the process of skill development. She says (p.45):

> Many individuals are hindered in performing a skilled movement simply because they do not have a large store of subroutines from which to draw, or the subroutines they do have are not effective. ..... If an adult has a limited number of subroutines, he must compensate for this lack of subroutines. If he cannot compensate and cannot discipline himself to learn new routines, his chances of executing a skilled movement are extremely poor.

This topic is referred to again in Chapter 6.

Summary

1. The teaching of skills is not just about passing on techniques to others. It is a complex procedure in which the teacher/coach must not only be technically articulate, but must also be aware of the learner's interests and aspirations, previous experience and how he/she relates to others. The sports coach/teacher must be a scientist, communicator, organiser, politician, social worker, friend, etc., and will only be effective if he/she balances the role of technician with these other roles.

2. Theories are generalisations about how things work and why things take place. They are based on observations and research and allow predictions of how things take place. Theories are not exhaustive nor are they complete or necessarily correct explanations of the phenomena they represent.

3. Theoretical knowledge is useful for a number of reasons, viz., it gives direction and structure to ones thinking and provides practical ideas based on sound, well-tested principles. Effective teaching and coaching is founded on the interplay between theoretical knowledge and practical experience.

4. The history of skill acquisition is punctuated by a number of landmarks: the observation and measurement of reaction time by early astronomers, the 'discovery' of plateaus and hierarchical learning by Bryan & Harter; the development of motor skills tests in the first half of the century; the emphasis on person-machine relationships through the advent of World War II; the efforts of particular researchers, e.g., Craik, Bartlett and Fitts which led to an increased interest in skill acquisition and a focus on topics such as anticipation, feedback, motor programming; research on motor memory; the information processing approach to the study of skilled performance.

5. Traditional theories of learning are split into Associative and Cognitive approaches. Association theories emphasise:
   a. Stimulus-response learning where development is a matter of linking specific stimuli with particular responses through repetition and reinforcement.
   b. Conditioning. Classical conditioning is the process whereby the learner links a new stimulus to a previous stimulus-response connection. Operant conditioning occurs when a response occurs more often through successive reinforcement. Behaviour shaping is the gradual refinement of a movement through reinforcement.
   c. Reinforcement. Immediate reinforcement is essential to the strengthening of responses.
   d. Repetition. Movements are more likely to be learned if they are satisfying to the learner. Repeated practice is important, but

only if there is positive reinforcement. Learning can only be expected if the person is physiologically and psychologically 'ready' to learn.

e.   Part learning. Complex problems are best broken down into smaller parts to yield short learning steps which can be linked together.

Cognitive theories emphasise:

a.   Importance of perception. Learning is based not only on cues in the display, but also the individual's perception of those cues. This in turn depends on the learner's self-concept, motivations, experience and expectations.

b.   Problem solving. The learner plays an active role in the learning process; searching and trying to understand how the cues and stimuli in the environment relate to the problem's solution. Insight, where the learner 'suddenly' finds a solution, marks an immediate and permanent stage in learning.

c.   Whole learning. Cognitive theories advocate that understanding and insight are only possible if the learner is confronted with the whole problem.

d.   Individual differences. Due acknowledgement is given to the individual nature of learning. The individual's 'self-concept' not only determines the course/manner of learning, but is itself altered through the learning process.

6.   Effective teaching takes advantage of principles from both approaches to learning and combines them with ideas from practical experience.

7.   Fitts's theory of skill learning divides the learning process into three broad areas: the cognitive, intermediate and autonomous stages.

8.   Adams' closed-loop theory focuses on the importance of feedback in the learning process. Feedback and knowledge of results is used to compare with the 'perceptual trace' as a way of identifying whether performance is successful.

9.   Schmidt's schema theory takes the view that people learn sets of 'rules' or schema which are used to organise movements. The theory has important implications for the manner in which practice is planned.

10. Information processing theory views the individual as a processor of information. Information enters from the outside world or from within the individual and passes through a series of stages such as perception and decision making, before movements occur.

Discussion questions

1.   It is said the fundamental role of the brain is to control movement. Think of two contrasting examples where information held in our memory manifests itself in physical movements. (e.g., smiling at a

joke; speaking to a friend)

2. Consider a simple action such as a basketball chest pass and describe those factors other than the technique which the teacher or coach must consider in order to produce an effective practice situation.
3. Think of a well known theory which you may have learned about at school (e.g., Newton's first law of motion) and show how it applies in the real world.
4. Researchers during the last war considered anticipation to be critical to skilled motor performance. Can you think of examples in your sport where anticipation takes place? Furthermore, can you identify a situation where as a player you attempt to make it difficult for your opponent to anticipate?
5. Have you ever experienced a 'plateau' in your own learning before your performance subsequently improved? If so, what do you think was happening to you during this period?
6. Isolate two clear examples from sport where success demands the timely execution of a movement response in reply to a given stimulus.
7. In what way would you interpret the skill of a rock climber as a matter of problem solving?
8. Take a specific situation in sport (say, a long pass in football) and examine the types of feedback the performer receives. Consider both internal and external forms.
9. Consider Schmidt's schema theory and the learning of rules. What kinds of rules would need to be acquired in activities such as orienteering and snooker?
10. What items does the tennis server need to perceive just before he serving the ball? One would be the position of his/her body in relation to the net. Name some others.
11. How would you characterise skilled performance? What are the criteria which define skill?

References

Adams, J.A. (1971) A closed loop theory of motor learning. *Journal of Motor Behavior*, **3**, 111–149.

Adams, J.A. (1976) Issues for a closed loop theory of motor learning. In Stelmach, G.E. (Ed.), *Motor control — Issues and trends*. London: Academic Press.

Bryan, W.L. and Harter, N. (1899) Studies in the telegraphic language: The acquisition of a hierarchy of habits. *Psychological Review*, **6**, 345–375.

Child, D. (1986) *Psychology and the teacher (4th Edition)* Eastbourne: Holt, Rinehart and Winston.

Fitts, P.M. (1964) Perceptual-motor skill learning. In Melton, A.W. (Ed.), *Categories of human learning*. New York: Academic Press.

Fitts, P.M. and Posner, M.I. (1967) *Human performance*. Belmont, California: Brooks/Cole.

Gleeson, G. (1984) *The coach in action*. Leeds: National Coaching Foundation.

Guthrie, E.R. (1952) *The psychology of learning*. New York: Harper & Row.

Holding, D.H. (Ed.) (1989) *Human skills (2nd. Ed.)*. Chichester: John Wiley.

Hill, W.F. (1980) *Learning: A survey of psychological interpretations (3rd. Ed.)*. London: Methuen.

Legge, D. (1970) *Skills*. Harmondsworth: Penguin.

Lewin, K. (1951) *Field theory of social science*. New York: Harper & Row.

Magill, R.A. (1990) Motor learning is meaningful for physical educators. *QUEST*, **42**, 126–133.

Martenuik, J.G. (1975) Information processing, channel capacity, learning stages and the acquisition of motor skill. In Whiting, H.T.A. (Ed.), *Readings in human performance*. London: Lepus Books.

Maynard, I. (1991) An understanding approach to the teaching of rugby union. *British Journal of Physical Education*, **22**, 1, 11–17.

Miller, J. (1978)*The body in question*. London: Jonathan Cape Ltd.

Robb, M.D. (1972) *The dynamics of motor-skill acquisition*. Englewood Cliffs, New Jersey: Prentice-Hall.

Schmidt, R.A. (1975) A schema theory of discrete motor skill learning. *Psychological Review*, **82**, 225–260.

Schmidt, R.A. (1976) The schema as a solution to some persistent problems in motor learning theory. In Stelmach, G.E. (Ed.), *Motor control — Issues and trends*. London: Academic Press.

Schmidt, R.A. (1982) *Motor control and learning*. Champaign, Illinois: Human Kinetics Publishers.

Smyth, M.M and Wing, A.M. (1984) *The psychology of human movement*. London: Academic Press.

Stelmach, G.E. (1976) *Motor control — Issues and trends*. London: Academic Press.

Stallings, L. (1982) *Motor learning from theory to practice*. London: C.V. Mosby.

Thorndike, E.L. (1927) The law of effect. *American Journal of Psychology*, **39**, 212–222.

Whiting, H.T.A. (1982) Skill in sport — A descriptive and prescriptive appraisal. In J.H. Salmela, J.T. Partington & T. Orlick (Eds.), *New paths to sport learning*. Ottawa: The Coaching Association of Canada.

Chapter 2

THE COMPLEXITY OF SKILL

Anyone for tennis?

Considering the amount of people involved in sport, the number and variety of sports in existence as well as the different motives that guide people to participate, it is hardly surprising that the analysis of skill — from whatever perspective — is a complex topic. Let's look at some of the reasons why people take part and try to improve their skill in sport. It is likely that such knowledge may help the teacher or coach guide and understand more effectively those in their charge.

There are a variety of reasons. Some people take part just to make friends. Skill improvement is secondary. Sport is a rich medium for meeting people and making friends. Sport also provides a means of improving fitness, losing weight, and so on. People join local walking clubs and aerobics classes simply to improve their health and fitness levels. Others may find they have a particular ability in sport and take part to nurture their inherent talents. Some people are good at those sports which emphasise the control of one's body (e.g., gymnastics, skiing, diving), whilst others tend to favour those sports which require making adjustments to an ever-changing display (as in soccer or volley-ball). By and large, people enjoy doing what they are good at and so participation provides much internal satisfaction. In this way sport contributes to self-concept and esteem in the eyes of others. And some people take part in sport for financial gain, national prestige, political gain and other esoteric reasons. It is probably difficult to assess the reasons why any one person enjoys sport. Some may not be able to articulate why they take part and for others there may be a number of reasons. The improvement of skill however, is central to the efforts of most. Let's now examine the major factors contributing to skill.

Skill and other things

In Chapter 1, the diverse nature of the coach's role was examined. It was suggested that on the whole, the coach does not simply attempt to pass on good techniques to people. In the same way, when people learn, they acquire more than techniques specific to their sport. It is useful to consider the model depicted in Figure 3 (overleaf). Although a simplification, it serves to highlight the complexity of human learning.

The affective dimension (to feel) concerns the emotional or attitudinal side of our personality. We reveal emotions when confronted with, say, a pleasant sight or hear of a terrible accident and we all respond differently to such situations. Similarly, we all have different aspirations in our professional lives and are motivated to pursue leisure interests in our free

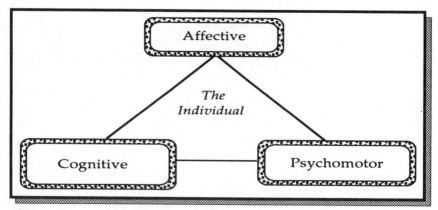

Figure 3: **A much simplified view showing three facets of the individual.**

time for varying reasons. The affective facet is, if you like, the 'qualitative' side of our personality. The cognitive dimension (to know) is concerned with our intellect and memory — how intelligent we are, how good we are at discussion and reasoning, how well we remember and converse with others. The last dimension — psychomotor (to do) — is concerned with our movements. Here again, we all differ in the manner in which we walk or run, the sports to which we are attracted and the level of performance we reach. This particular categorisation is only one of many. Gagne (1977), for example, describes a five-way categorisation which is also useful. In most classifications of this kind, motor skills are given particular recognition.

The point in describing this three-way approach is to reinforce the complexity of skill learning. Performing well in sport demands more than just acquiring a repertoire of movement patterns. To be good demands the athlete knows and understands the rules of the sport, understands the value and nature of complex strategies, and perhaps keeps a precise log of training and also knows something of the sport's history. These are all intellectual elements which the athlete may take on board and there will be many other facets too.

Excellence also depends on mental attitude, setting correct goals, dedication and application to hard training, sportsmanship, motivation, the need to achieve and, possibly, the 'right' sort of personality, etc.. Technology plays its part too and McCarthy (1990) has recently shown ways in which performance in a number of sports can be enhanced through improvements in equipment design, materials, and so on. The affective dimension is without doubt a critical ingredient in sport and one which has taken on much greater prominence in sport during the last decade through the influence of sport psychology. Both athlete and coach must be aware of cognitive and attitudinal aspects if the athlete is to meet his/her potential.

Finally, the learner acquires the techniques of his/her sport; the precise movement patterns which if executed at the right time and in the right manner reveal fluent, skilled performance. Skilled performance then, is an interplay between attitudes, knowledge and movements. Both learner and teacher must be fully aware of these ingredients if success, enjoyment and excellence are to be achieved. This is highlighted in a comment from John Shedden, the English National Skiing Coach (quoted in Sharp, 1986). He says:

> There is a general misconception that skill is essentially technical excellence and whilst it's not possible to be skilled without a high level of technical excellence, it's also very important for the learner to realise that the control of his body is important, but so is the control of his emotions and the ability of his body to carry out the tasks that are set which requires certain levels of fitness. Therefore, skill is a continuous interplay between the technical ability of the skier, the emotions of the skier, the perceptions and judgments that skier can make and the fitness or the degree of preparedness that the skier possesses. Skill is developed therefore by attending to all of these things either in turn or combinations of one or the other.

A definition of skill

Let us now focus on the psychomotor dimension of the model in the previous figure and examine what we mean by skill and skill acquisition. The word skill has many uses and is used by the layperson as well as sports coaches and teachers. We talk about the skill of a surgeon or a skilled darts player. We refer to a person who speaks many languages as a skilled linguist. Someone who communicates easily with people and who makes friends readily could be said to possess good social skills. There is a common element in all these examples but, if we are not to be confused or misunderstood, we should tease out what we really mean by skill. Within the context of sport the word skill is used in several ways:

- when referring to a specific act or sequence of movements such as a chest pass in basketball, a somersault in gymnastics or a snowplough turn in skiing;
- to define the level of performance of an individual or team. For example, a volleyball team may play at district level or an athlete may be a good club runner. In this context an international athlete would be considered more skilled than a club-standard athlete;
- in the more specific context of high level performance. In this case, one is either skilled or not skilled. Thus, a person is considered to be skilled only if, for example, he/she competes at Olympic level.

Given that there exist different interpretations of skill, the present text adopts the view that skill is something which belongs to the individual. It is not something which resides outside the person in the form of, say, a physical movement. Rather, skill is something which helps the link between intention and action. We can be more precise and say that skill satisfies four criteria. Let us examine these criteria and then follow by showing how this knowledge can help the coach and teacher.

1.   Firstly, skill results in actions which have a clear end result. Skill is goal-directed. Thus, one learns to spike a volleyball in order to reduce the time for the opposition to play a return shot. Or, one learns to navigate in a woodland area so as to develop confidence in more mountainous terrain. Similarly, one may learn to swim in order to meet friends or achieve fitness. Skill has direction and purpose.

2.   Secondly, skill is a learned characteristic. Skill requires practice and experience for proficiency. This means that skill is not acquired through hereditary influences. It also follows that skill improvement is not based on changes in age or increased fitness. A person's performance may improve because they develop their flexibility (say, in gymnastics), but it would be wrong to say that skill learning has taken place. Skill requires physical practice and other kinds of related experiences such as observation and feedback for improvements to occur. Skill acquisition takes place in the brain and is a relatively permanent state of affairs, unlike say flexibility or endurance which are free to fluctuate depending on how fit the player is.

3.   Thirdly, skill results in movements which are economic and efficient in terms of their energy and time outlay. Skilled action is not clumsy to the eye. There are cases of good performers who look clumsy in the way they move (e.g., a soccer player may move awkwardly but still be an effective goal scorer) but, by and large, skilled action is pleasing to see, well-timed, consistent, co-ordinated, and precisely measured, and so on.

4.   Finally, skilled activity is the end result of a whole chain of central nervous system activity. For example, a skilled netball player needs to select and absorb information about the game, opponents and team mates. When in possession of the ball she needs to decide what action to take. This will depend on the score in the game, her position on court, the position of other players, and so on. Only when her brain has processed such information can she initiate the most appropriate action. How skilled that action is, will depend on the success of the preceding nervous activity as well as the efficiency of the resulting movements. An illustration of this overall view of skill is the example of a squash player who may well be able to 'read' the game and know what shots to play but, through lack of co-ordination, fails to make the right moves. Similarly, an aspiring soccer player may be a very competent 'juggler' of the ball but lack the perceptive awareness and decision making ability to translate such skills into the game proper. Shedden (quoted in

Sharp, 1986) expresses this very well when describing skiing:

> A skilful skier is one who has learned techniques, but more than that, one who can use those techniques by making sound judgements about his own level of performance on that day, about his own emotional disposition to the snow conditions and about the nature of the surface on which he is skiing — the snow textures and so on — in order to make the technical ability that he has effective.

Skill, therefore, is not just about carrying out particular movements. It is much broader than this and involves the brain carrying out a number of tasks all of which have to be executed successfully. The model depicted in Figure 4 illustrates this idea.

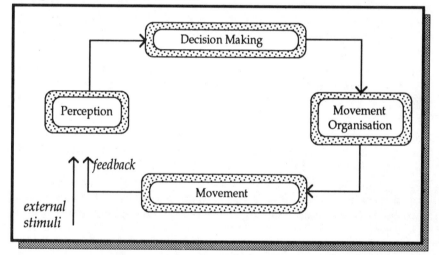

Figure 4: **A model of human performance. In this model the individual receives information from internal and external sources which has to be perceived and made sense of. Based on this input, the person decides what to do and begins to plan actions accordingly. Resulting movements produce feedback information which, combined with outside data, completes the cycle of information-processing.**

A definition of skill learning

Before looking at some of the implications of these points we must define what is meant by skill acquisition or skill learning. Learning is reflected in a change in performance. We say that a person has learned something if their performance shows improvement from one occasion to the next. A young javelin thrower may improve from throwing, say, 25 metres to 30 metres. Such an improvement must be stable and relatively permanent and not just a transient increase caused, for example, by a change in fitness level or improvement in health. Moreover, maturational or developmental changes which may predispose a learner to better performance (e.g., increases in body weight, development of the central nervous system) are not responsible for learning. Learning takes place through practice and experience.

It is worth mentioning here that whilst learning is recognised by observing changes in a learner's performance over time, lack of change does not imply learning is not taking place! This stems from what has already been said about the complexity of skill and how skilled perform-ance depends not only on the ability to execute good technique but also the capacity to perceive, attend, make decisions, anticipate, and so on. The learner may well be making internal changes with regard to these elements (e.g., learning to recognise which cues to attend to) but they are insufficiently developed to result in significant technical improvement. This kind of reasoning accounts very well for the common experience of 'plateaus' in learning. There are other reasons which will be dealt with when talking about motivation later on (see Chapter 7).

It is also worth mentioning that a number of expressions have been used to describe skill learning. Expressions such as motor skill acquisition, perceptual-motor learning, psychomotor learning and motor learning all mean essentially the same thing. The expression 'motor learning' tends to undermine the complexity of skill acquisition and suggests that it is just concerned with motor actions: i.e., techniques. Different authors have taken account of perception and the important link between perceptual and motor elements to coin the expression 'perceptual-motor skill'. Skill acquisition seems to be the most appropriate term.

Implications

What are the implications of these four criteria for coaching and learning? Let us take each one in turn.

Goal direction

If skill is goal directed and aimed at achieving specific results, then the instructor must be aware of the goal and generally speaking so too must the learner. Both parties must have a clear idea why a movement or technique is being practised and how it fits into a broader context. This means that the coach or teacher must plan ahead with clear direction in his/her training and instructional work. Similarly, the learner must be made aware — if it is not obvious — of the reasons why he/she is practising certain things and why training is vital. Too often the reason for doing things is overlooked by the coach who, perhaps because he or she is wrapped up in his or her subject, assumes the learner knows what the objective is. An example of this type of problem would be what might be called the 'skiing by numbers' approach to teaching beginners to ski.

Often, instructors break down each required movement into its constituent parts without giving the learner a chance to appreciate the overall effect of the sequence of movements. This can be solved by talking to learners and expressing the reasons for breaking actions down into smaller parts. An example from badminton illustrates this point. On introducing a backhand clear to learners, the coach could indicate why this is a good stroke to add to their repertoire. He could talk about the need to force opponents to the backcourt so as to gain extra time for recovery. The coach could illustrate this by setting up practice of a low drive and a high clear with a view to comparing the relative recovery times to base. This would reinforce the importance of the movement and help motivate the learner to greater effort.

Learning

We shall elaborate on this point later but at this stage it is sufficient to point out two things. Firstly, the coach must consider what are the correct kinds of learning experiences needed to improve skill. He must, for example, devise the correct type and length of physical practice for the learner. How long should the gymnast practise a routine on the rings and how many unsuccessful attempts should he/she be allowed to make before moving onto something different? Should techniques be treated as 'wholes' or broken down into smaller parts? Further, how should the amount of time spent actually practising be balanced with different experiences such as watching others perform, discussing problems with fellow learners, critically evaluating ones own skill, mentally rehearsing and so on. Experiences such as these are vital to learning. The old adage "practice makes perfect" is not always correct. Valid practice must be mixed with other experiences and for different learners in different ways.

Secondly, the coach must be sure that learning really has taken place. Learning cannot be assumed to take place simply because the learner understands what is to be done and is given half an hour to practice. The learner may perform well today but not the next time the action is attempted. Learning is recognised by a permanent change in performance which remains relatively stable over time. The coach must be convinced that learning is taking place and this will involve not only structuring repeated practice, but also monitoring and evaluating progress in some way. Evaluation might be through direct visual observation or through more objective means such as using a skill or fitness test or video-taping the learner or encouraging the learner to keep a log book which is monitored by the teacher or coach from time to time.

Efficiency

If skilled movement meets certain criteria concerned with effectiveness and economy of action then the coach must know what constitutes "good" performance. Coaches and teachers (perhaps to a lesser degree) must be technically articulate. Judges in any competitive sport where technique is evaluated — e.g., gymnastics or ice skating — know what skilled movement looks like and are able to make assessments of good and bad performance very quickly. They are able to compare what they see with an internal memory of the correct performance and spot errors immediately. Coaches may not need to be quite so speedy in their judgements, but they must be accurate. Only then will they be able to tell whether the learner is improving or consolidating a bad habit and thus be in a position to give feedback enabling learning to continue. The process of error detection and correction and the techniques available are considered in Chapter 4.

Before leaving the matter of skill efficiency it should be understood that skilled movements are not always so rigid and well-defined that a strict movement pattern should be followed in a precisely-executed manner. The environment in which we live is relatively 'forgiving'. Skilled movement can be flexible in that a small degree of 'error' is usually possible whilst still allowing success. For example, the timing of catching a ball can be a little late or early but the ball will still be held. Research has shown that when catching a lawn tennis ball the catcher can afford to time the catch within a time band of approximately 20 msecs.. Figure 5 illustrates this principle.

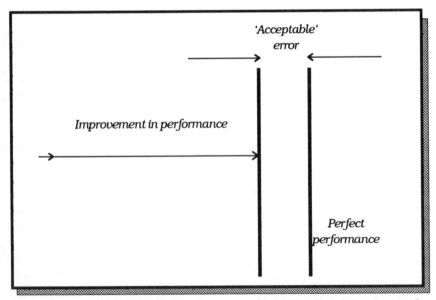

Figure 5:   **Learning may be viewed as a gradual striving towards perfect performance. The final margin of error will depend on many things including the stage of learning and characteristics of the task. Not all tasks demand perfect performance: e.g., ball-catching error tolerance is in the order of centiseconds.**

Using the same principle, we can see that Olympic and club class athletes might well make the same general movement, but their technique and therefore the ultimate quality of that movement will be different. It is the same general movement but the technique will be different. The same could be said for many other actions (e.g., tennis serve, triple jump, chest pass, sweep stroke in canoeing). The implication here is that the coach must teach and expect performance from people which is appropriate to their level of competence. It could be harmful for example, to expect novice high jumpers to practise a Fosbury flop as their first technique. An easier/ less dangerous technique such as the western roll might be more appropriate. The same principle applies to individuals who differ in their body shape or fitness levels. A person's physical make-up may well dictate the manner in which they execute a movement. The sensitive coach acknowledges this by expecting performance only within the physical constraints of the learner's make-up.

Central nervous system processing

This final point is very important. The way in which movement is carried out is just the final outcome of what may be considered to be a whole chain of processes including sensing and perceiving information, attending to the right things, making decisions at the correct time and anticipating when a movement is required. To be proficient, a player has to be skilled not only in carrying out movements, but also skilled in these unseen activities which take place in the brain before the movement is executed. Let us give some examples of this. A rock climber ascending a new route must use the body in a manner which is mechanically efficient and 'matched' to fit the shape of the rock. He/she must also use knowledge of the rock to identify possible hand and footholds and to anticipate the next combination of moves which will provide a balanced position. It is said that a rock climber 'climbs with the eyes'. Perceptual skills are needed as well as motor skills, and if proficient in all aspects the climber will be able to execute skilled movements and be seen by others to move skilfully. To take another example, consider a child learning to play soccer. Initially he/she will grapple with the physical movements of kicking, trapping the ball, etc., as well as the problem of learning rules and basic tactics such as where to pass the ball, who to pass it to and when to release it. To the beginner, there are perceptual, decision-making and motor elements to worry about. As the child becomes more skilled, then action depends less on ball control and trapping ability, etc., and more on cognitive aspects such as tactics, decision making, confusing the opposition, and so on. This example demonstrates not only the unseen, internal factors involved in skill but also indicates how their relative balance may alter through learning.

Thus, different skill levels present different kinds of problems. Some aspects of skill may require emphasis at one stage of learning whilst others take over at a later stage. This is an issue about which the coach or teacher needs to be fully aware, for it is only logical that he/she presents to the learner skills and ideas which are pertinent to that learner's level of expertise and understanding. Too often, instructors tend to get bogged down with the techniques of their sport at the expense of other important aspects. They must be aware of which points to emphasise, which cues to draw attention to and which techniques to introduce at each stage of development. This is a topic which we will return to in Chapter 5 when dealing with how to break complex actions down into smaller parts.

Skills and techniques

It should be clear from what has already been said that there is a difference between skills and techniques. Techniques describe movement patterns. When you watch someone perform you observe techniques being executed. Techniques reside outside the performer and until he or she moves there is no way of knowing if technique is good or bad. Techniques lend themselves to ease of measurement. A video or cine film can be analysed to yield for example, precise data on temporal or spatial accuracy and patterning. This kind of analysis would be of particular interest to the biomechanist.

Skills are more than techniques. They are concerned with the application of good techniques at the correct time. A player may have a repertoire of good techniques (e.g., the expert football juggler), but be unable to use them in the game situation. Such a person would not be skilled. As already emphasised, it is vital the learning process shows the learner how and when to apply techniques.

A word which sometimes causes confusion is the word *ability*. We often refer to an able or skilled person and we may say that someone has lots of abilities. The words skill and ability are frequently used interchangeably. To clarify the exact meaning, it is useful to think of an ability as something which the learner possesses (as distinct from techniques which, as we have noted above, happen outside the person), and which is more general than skill. In addition, abilities should be thought of as inherited whereas skill is learned. Abilities are enduring characteristics which underlie a person's potential to acquire skill in one sport or another. It is suggested that to be skilful, say in gymnastics, the individual must possess a given profile of underlying abilities. In the case of gymnastics we might list such abilities as kinesthetic awareness (sensitivity to movement via internal feelings within the muscles and joints), manual dexterity (use of the hands and arms to carry out fine movements) and co-ordination (the capacity to balance when moving quickly or poised in a still position).

The important thing to note here is that such abilities are not specific to gymnastics; they may be intrinsic to other sports also. Theoretically, it is possible to define the underlying abilities which contribute to any sport, but this is an area of research which has proved to be very difficult to assess. If it were possible to do this, then it could be reasoned that instruction should be devoted to enhancing people's abilities rather than skill in particular sports. In this way, not only would time be saved but, learners might be more able to transfer their learning between sports which share common abilities. This kind of thinking applies in movement education where underlying movement concepts such as timing and flow are developed in the belief they will transfer to subsequent sports. More research is needed on this matter.

One topic which has received support from research is the idea that abilities important in early learning may not be the same as those required later. It is thought that the 'structure' or profile of abilities required in a particular sport changes as the learner becomes more competent. This idea would account for the common example of the youngster who 'stars' early on, but never achieves his/her expected performance: he/she possesses the correct mix of abilities as a beginner but not as an expert. We shall return to this issue in a later chapter when looking at teaching beginners and experts and also when considering the topic of task analysis. Figure 6 summarises the relationship between skill, ability and techniques. The interested reader may wish to refer to Fleishman (1964) which, although a dated text, provides valuable insight to the relationship between skill and abilities.

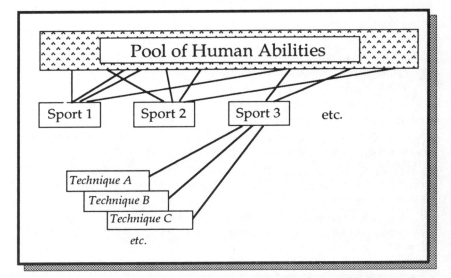

Figure 6: The hierarchical relationship between abilities, skill and technique. Every individual possesses a particular pool of abilities refined to a lesser or greater degree. Particular sports demand the availability of a given profile of abilities for success. In turn, each sport reflects itself in a number of defined techniques.

Summary

1. Skill is defined by four criteria. It is goal-directed. It is learned. Skill results in actions which are efficient in terms of their outlay in energy/time. Skill involves much 'internal processing' as well as physical action.
2. Learners should be directed to the aims of their learning experience and informed about why they are practising or training in certain ways.
3. Physical practice is only one way in which the learner acquires skill and knowledge. Other experiences such as watching athletes perform, viewing video film of themselves in action, mental practice, etc., may be equally important.
4. The performance of learners should be monitored in order to evaluate whether or not learning is taking place.
5. The coach/teacher should know what skilled performance looks like and be able to detect and correct errors. Observation ability is based on technical knowledge, coaching/teaching experience as well as personal experience in sport.
6. It should be acknowledged that different people will perform the same movement in different ways and allowance should be made for variations in technique between people.
7. Skill is relative in the sense that whilst two people may perform competently at their particular level of play (e.g., Olympic or club) they may both be judged as skilled players by their respective colleagues.
8. The coach and teacher should know what are the important ingredients which contribute to skill. They should understand what are the perceptual aspects (e.g., what information to attend to, what information to ignore), the decision making aspects (e.g., when to time an action, how many ways of executing movements) as well as the motor aspects (nature of the movement pattern, importance of feedback). In addition, it should be clear when is the appropriate time for each element to be introduced to the learner.
9. Techniques are movement patterns. Skill reflects itself in good technique. Abilities, which are enduring, inherited qualities form the basis of skill. To be skilled and hence demonstrate good technique requires the possession of appropriate underlying abilities.

Discussion questions

1. Identify two sports which emphasise perception and decision making, and technique and movement execution respectively.
2. Take a particular sport and identify some elements which should be learned before others. If there is no order of introduction, indicate why not.

3. What methods are available for getting across the idea of these elements, without employing actual physical practice?
4. What objective procedures (e.g., tests) could you employ to verify skill improvement?
5. Take a particular technique from the sport chosen in 1, and describe clearly the difference seen when comparing the action performed correctly and performed incorrectly.
6. Are there any elements of the sport which the learner concentrates on initially but later go unnoticed?
7. To what extent do you think the skill of your players/performers is limited by their age, sex and lack of say, strength?.
8. It is sometimes said that a person who has reached a high level of personal performance in their sport does not necessarily make a good coach! It is reasoned that the expert may forget the problems and issues relevant to early learning and attempt to impose high level technique and concepts on the learner too early. Comment on this argument from your own perspective.
9. Take another technique and identify the external information the performer needs in order to carry out the action successfully.

References

Fleishman, E.A. (1964) *The structure and measurement of physical fitness.* Englewood Cliffs, New Jersey: Prentice Hall.

Gagne, R.M. (1977) *The conditions of learning (3rd. Ed.).* New York: Holt, Rinehart & Winston.

McCarthy, J. (1990) *Journal of the Canadian Association for Health, Physical Education and Recreation,* **56**, 3, 34-35.

Shedden, J. Quoted in Sharp, R.H. (1986) *Acquiring skill — Module 1.* Edinburgh: Scottish Sports Council.

Chapter 3

PROVIDING INFORMATION TO LEARNERS

Introduction

Feedback is information received by the learner during/after he or she has attempted a skilled movement. However, although it is recognised that feedback is one of the most important aids to learning, the learner must be in receipt of accurate information before that movement is attempted. This chapter focuses on that part of the instructional process concerned with the provision of information, advice and knowledge to the learner in advance of actual practice.

It is useful to start by distinguishing between practice and training. For the purposes of the present discussion training is the process of executing a movement with the help or guidance from an outside source such as a coach or teacher. Practice on the other hand involves going through a movement without any kind of outside help. Both situations have a part to play in skill learning for there are times when the learner needs advice from the coach and other times when either it is unavailable or simply not required. Let us look at practice for a moment. There are a number of disadvantages associated with practice. In the first place, learning may be very much a trial and error affair. Without input from the coach the learners only have their own models of skill to use as a basis for error correction — and it may well be wrong. As a result, errors may build up which, if unnoticed, may give rise to the learning and consolidation of bad habits. An additional problem is that as soon as the habits are recognised, practice time and effort is required not only to learn the correct movements, but also to 'unlearn' the faulty ones. These points are raised by Hickey, a boxing coach (quoted in Sharp, 1986):

> Uncoached practice is bad. Not just because of the time wasted and perhaps the high risk of injury, but also what's going to happen is that bad habits will be formed. So with uncoached practice what will happen is that the technique will be grooved which is perhaps mechanically unsound, which may not cause problems in the early stages but once the boxer goes into competition at the higher echelons he will certainly have problems simply because he was allowed too much free time. Coaching should be structured. Practices must be pointed and precise and there should be no question of a boxer doing his own thing literally.

A second problem of practice alone is that the process encourages methods which bring success very quickly, but because they are often technically unsound, skill level remains mediocre. Coupled with the absence of outside praise and corrective advice, the scene is set for little or no progress, frustration and possible dropout by the learner from the sport. This paints a rather gloomy picture of practice, but it would be wrong to think it has no place. Many people are happy to practice alone or with their friends in the complete knowledge they will improve very little. And of course many top athletes work alone improving their skill and levels of fitness. There is a very big difference, however, with experienced performers. They are better able to make adjustments to their performance because they have an internal model of skill which is correct. Also, they are able to interpret their own feedback and self analyse more precisely. This is based in large part on the accumulation of advice and guidance from other people. We shall examine the value of practice later but for the present we need to look at the methods of guidance available to the coach.

Methods of Guidance

A simple way of categorising methods of guidance is to examine the various ways we receive information. We possess a number of senses and some are more important than others. The obvious ones are vision, audition, kinesthesis and touch. It seems unlikely that the coach would take advantage of the remaining senses of smell and taste. There are a number of interesting things about the way in which our senses are structured and function. One feature is that whilst they are physiologically different and respond to distinctly different kinds of energy (e.g., the eyes respond to light energy whilst the ears respond to mechanical energy) they can present to the brain the same information. To give a rather dramatic example of this, suppose a pig walked into your living room! You would clearly recognise that it was a pig by using any single sense. Thus you would be able to see that it was pig. You would smell that it was pig. You could tell from the noises it made that it was a pig. By feeling its body contours (with your eyes closed) you would identify that it was a pig and perhaps if you were to take a bite then you would also identify the characteristic taste of a pig. The implication of this for learning is that it makes it possible for the coach to respond to individual differences between people by presenting the same thing in different ways. This is useful because people seem to have preferred ways of picking up information: i.e., some prefer to see a demonstration whilst others may prefer a detailed verbal account. Another important thing about the senses is the manner in which they interact with one another. The observation that taste seems to go when you have a cold points to the fact that taste is a function of both taste and smell. Similarly, if watching television and there is a fault in transmission such that either sound or vision is lost, then the viewer is often left extremely frustrated and misses vital information.

It follows that complete perception is only possible if both vision and audition are present together. This fact also has important implications for learning for it allows the coach to use a variety of presentation techniques in combination in order to get messages across to learners. So, if a learner fails to understand through watching a demonstration and listening to a brief explanation, he/she may benefit from say a longer description coupled with some form of manual assistance. Another person may learn best by just watching a video of an expert performer and feeling the movements through guidance from the coach. The coach can thus 'mix and match', as it were, a variety of methods to appeal to individual people.

Visual Guidance

Harrison and Blakemore (1989) have estimated that about 83% of all learning occurs through showing people what to do, 11% through hearing and 6% through other senses. Although it is debatable whether these kinds of figures are really accurate they do support a common belief that the visual sense is probably the most dominant way in which we communicate with the outside world. Much evidence supports this statement. It is not surprising therefore that one of the most common techniques used in teaching and coaching is visual guidance. Shedden (quoted in Sharp, 1986) underlines this point in the following comments:

> One of the most important forms of information is visual information and this is especially true of children. But even for adults, to have an impression of what the movements look like in motion, very often from a totally different viewpoint than the demonstrator would give if he were standing with the group, is important. This can be given by film or by video-tape presentation. Video-tape is also very good for allowing performers to see themselves and therefore match their own visual impression of themselves with the ideal visual model. The most common means of communicating to a beginner in skiing what to do is the use of a demonstration — the ski instructor or coach demonstrates to the beginner. As the beginner gets more expert, the use of demonstration becomes more and more limited and information from other sources is more desirable.

Shedden points to a number of different visual guidance methods which can be categorised in the following way:
- Demonstrations
- Use of visual materials (e.g., wallcharts, video)
- Re-structuring of the display.

Let us take each one in turn.

Demonstrations

The aim of a demonstration is to present to the learner a visual model which he/she can then copy. Demonstrations take advantage of a very powerful principle in learning: learning by imitation. A rich body of literature shows that people do learn by imitating others and almost everyone can think of examples where this has happened. Young children are especially good at picking things up very speedily although, as many teachers and parents will know, they are equally adept at learning things they shouldn't!

Demonstrations are very efficient in terms of time. They offer an immediate picture and also save the coach the problem of expressing the task in words, which could confuse the learner. The saying 'a picture paints a thousand words' is especially true when it comes to describing complex movements. Demonstrations have a place at all stages of learning. A demonstration gives the novice a general idea of what is required and is intuitively more appealing than, say, a lengthy talk. The fact that it takes place in real time and in the immediate vicinity of the learner adds to its general impact and value in motivating the beginner. A demonstration for the expert is useful in highlighting specific points — say, the manner in which the bowler moves the hand when imparting spin to the ball — which could not be examined in any other practical way. Demonstrations also allow advantage to be taken of other people's skills and expertise. For example, if the coach or teacher cannot perform then it may be possible for someone else — perhaps one of the learners — to show the rest how the movement is carried out. Coaches are in a particularly advantageous position here because attention can be drawn to specific points in the demonstration which would be impossible if they were performing themselves. Demonstrations by learners with particular weaknesses is also a useful technique if handled carefully and can be used to highlight the differences between good and bad technique.

These are some of the advantages, but demonstrations are not always the panacea they are assumed to be. Social learning theory (e.g., Bandura, 1969) indicates that 'observational learning' only occurs if the learner:

- attends to the demonstration
- remembers the information conveyed by the demonstration until he/she practises
- possesses the ability to reproduce the movements, and
- has the motivation to practise.

With these in mind, it should not be assumed that demonstrations work automatically. Careful thought must be given to the timing, nature and emphasis of a demonstration. The learner has to make a 'transformation' from what the eyes tell him to what the muscles must do. It does not follow that the learner can convert automatically a visual image into a physical movement. The value of demonstrations depends on a number of points.

1. The demonstration must be relevant to the needs of the learner and must be pitched at the correct level. A teaching manual on skill learning tells how a bricklayer has three different kinds of demonstration — a fast one, a slow one and one for the benefit of apprentices. The same must also hold true in sport where the coach or teacher should tailor the precision and intention of the demonstration to suit the aspiration and skill level of those in his/her charge. A demonstration which, for example, uses a star performer may display too high a level of expertise which is not only unattainable but which also discourages the learner from trying. Newell, Morris and Scully (1985) also suggest that demonstrations in early learning only have temporary value because practice and feedback provide much more important sources of information.

2. Demonstrations must be accurate and must emphasise the required point. Demonstrations may be executed incorrectly and it is always possible that demonstrations given by the coach run the risk of revealing personal errors they are unaware of and of presenting too much detail. In contrast, a demonstration given by someone else allows the coach to monitor possible faults as well as focus on just the relevant points. The nature of demonstration also depends on the level of learning. This is highlighted by Jameson (quoted in Sharp, 1986) in relation to dinghy sailing:

> Demonstration takes place at two levels. In teaching beginners the instructor actually gets into the boat and demonstrates movements before handing the helm over to the beginner. He then tries and so on. In race training, it's not possible to do this because the relationship and the movements between helm and crew are very fine and the only way that demonstrations can be done here is by using members of a particular squad or possibly bringing in a sailor from a higher level to come in and demonstrate.

A vital point is that learners should be left to watch demonstrations without having to listen to the coach simultaneously. In the knowledge that people can only attend fully to one thing at a time, it is good practice for the coach to talk through the movement and highlight the points to observe in advance of the demonstration, then allow unhindered observation afterwards. For example, in coaching a forward somersault on the trampoline, the coach might talk about the need to move the hips behind the vertical and then tell the learner to watch the hips only during the demonstration. This should direct the learner's attention away from irrelevant aspects of the movement and allow concentration during the demonstration of hip displacement alone. It is also vital to repeat demonstrations to make sure everyone has seen and to confirm the point has been understood. Research shows that repeated demonstrations help reinforce ideas.

They also allow anyone who missed information on the first demonstration to 'catch up'.

3. A point related to accuracy concerns the exact nature of the model upon which a demonstration is based. Is the model appropriate for the learners in question? Is it pitched at the right level? Is it correct? An example illustrates this last point. In the sphere of women's gymnastics, recent video film revealed how some Eastern European performers displayed an upstart technique which differed quite markedly from the traditional technique. On analysis, it turned out the new technique was more efficient in terms of its energy outlay when compared with the accepted method (Kerwin & Sprunt, 1988). It is possible this improved technique will be used as a model for all future gymnasts. The point about models (and hence demonstrations) is that they must be seen as things which change over time and alter with the learner in question and also his/her stage of learning as well as changes to equipment, technology and technique efficiency (e.g., Fosbury Flop). The good teacher recognises the need to adapt with regard to changes in the sport and differences between individual learners. This aspect is discussed again in Chapter 6.

4. A fourth aspect concerns positioning of the learner in relation to the demonstration. To take the trampoline example just cited, it would be pointless standing people around the trampoline because those standing to the front and rear of the performer would not see any hip movement. Only those positioned laterally would observe the point being made by the coach. The same goes for demonstrations which are not symmetrical. For example, in showing a golf swing or how to tie a climbing knot, the person demonstrating should consider whether it is best to face the learner so revealing a mirror image of the movement, or turn around to present the movement proper — albeit slightly obscured. Therefore, angular positioning on the part of the demonstrator is important. Other related considerations are distance the learner is from the demonstration (consider the ski instructor mentioned before who runs the risk of moving away very quickly from the group) and obstructions such as lighting and background texture which could render observation very poor.

5. Finally, demonstrations provide a good basis for discussion. The coach should encourage question and answer as a way of solving uncertainties in the learner's mind. It is insufficient to provide a demonstration followed by practice without first ascertaining whether learners have fully understood and know what to do next. And lastly, it is vital the coach does not spend too much time on personal demonstrations — after all, it is the learner who is there to improve and not the coach!

Visual materials

Wallcharts, colour slides, diagrams, three-dimensional models, etc., are initially attractive and may serve to enhance the learning environment but their static nature soon renders them redundant (think of a living room clock whose constant tick soon disappears from attention). Some research has shown that static displays convey little or no information about the movements to be performed (e.g., Barclay, Cutting & Kozlowski, 1978). They may help focus attention on a technical point from time to time but, by and large, their value is very limited. Dynamic media such as film loops and especially video recordings of experts or learners are shown to be much more beneficial. Both are useful if the coach cannot give a competent demonstration and slow motion facilities reveals precise form which would be missed in a real time demonstration. With regard to the latter however, Scully (1988) has shown that slow motion replays of movement can be a very limited source of information. They may indicate 'relative' movement between body segments, but they provide nothing about absolute movement.

Let us focus on the use of video for a moment. Video is used increasingly by coaches as a medium for demonstration and the provision of feedback. Recent research shows however, that demonstrations using this medium are only effective if certain conditions are met. Firstly, the learner's attention must be directed verbally to vital points in the demonstration. It is no good allowing people to simply watch a video without any kind of intervention or analysis by the coach/teacher or else it becomes just an opportunity for enjoyment alone — or possibly sleep on the part of those watching! Secondly, the learner must be given an opportunity to practise before his/her memory of the points made in the video has faded. This at least suggests the showing must be very brief. Thirdly, the learner must possess the ability to reproduce the desired action shown in the demonstration — the point about relevance was made at the beginning of this chapter. If the object is to present a model to be copied then the model must be attainable. Fourthly, repetitive use of the video is necessary for there to be any significant performance gains. This may involve alternate use of practice and observation to ensure the learner has fully appreciated what is required. And lastly, the learner must be motivated to reproduce the action. He/she must 'want' to understand and learn new things. The coach may have the best will in the world but if the coach's attitude is wrong, if attainable goals have not been set and established a purposeful atmosphere, then learners may not wish to follow the coach's advice. These issues and others related to goal-setting and motivation are elaborated in Chapter 7.

Display changes

The next chapter examines the topic of feedback. One of the difficulties experienced by the learner is that frequently there is simply too much feedback. The problem for both learner and teacher is how to contain the overload of information which produces such a confusing picture for the learner. The problem of information overload is also a potential threat when providing guidance to the learner. One way around this is to highlight or enhance important visual cues by changing the display in some way. This technique is used for example, in table tennis, cricket and lawn tennis where sight screens make it easier for the player to spot the ball against what might otherwise be a confusing background. Similarly, the umpire's decision-making in cricket is assisted through the use of a white ball and coloured pads. And recently, televised squash has improved dramatically through the use of light-reflecting balls which make it much simpler for the viewer to spot the ball against the walls. The same principle can be used to help learners concentrate on particular aspects in the display. For example, the use of fluorescent volleyballs or tennis balls makes it easier to spot the ball's position and speed in flight. In gymnastics the drawing of chalk marks on the floor helps to direct hand placement and direction during a floor sequence. And in lawn tennis it helps the would-be server to aim the ball accurately when the floor has been chalked or marked in a way which provides a target. In a similar way, the actually playing area can be manipulated to encourage certain techniques. For example, a soccer pitch can be reduced in length to encourage passing skills; a badminton court can be reduced in width to focus attention on particular shots such as lobs and clears. Scully (1988) even suggests that videos can be edited to highlight particular joint movements by adding verbal cues at the appropriate moment or by affixing contrasting tape to the joints in question if using a live demonstration or creating one's own video.

In many sports the coach/teacher can help the learner by emphasising the use of existing visual points of reference in the display. For example, the black square on the basketball backboard can be used as a target when shooting. And in the front crawl, the black line which finishes in a 'T' just before the wall can be used as a reference for beginning a tumble turn.

Methods such as these are potentially very useful and can be applied to most sports, but their use demands some imagination and initiative on the part of the coach. They seem to have particular benefit in 'one-off' situations when assisting particular learners overcome a difficult problem.

Verbal guidance

Let us now move onto the topic of verbal guidance. It cannot be denied that talking to people and telling them what to do is important, but exactly what purpose does it serve? It seems that verbal instructions can convey essentially two things:

- What the action or task actually is. That is, what it looks like in terms of its technical specification and what its objectives are. A coach may

explain for example, what a volleypass looks like and when/why it should be used.
- How the learner is able to carry out the movement. The coach could describe what the learner must do in order to volley the ball and what it feels like when done correctly.

The first point is really a straight description of the movement. It would appear that coaches and teachers are very good at doing this. As long as they have an accurate model it is not too difficult to tell the learner what to do — although it might be a rather lengthy description. The second point is concerned with explanation and is arguably the more complex of the two, requiring a much more in-depth knowledge of the action and its constituent parts. An example from trampolining illustrates these points very well. It is quite easy to describe a seat drop and a front drop in terms of their spatial requirements — perhaps a demonstration or video would enhance a description to the learner, but it is more difficult to isolate the important cues and actions and express them in a way which allows the learner to link the two movements together. In this example, the link is made by telling the learner to 'move the head to the toes' as he/she leaves the bed from the seat drop. It is important to note that comments such as these may not comprise part of the individual movements and they may not form part of the technical descriptions. In large part, instructions which tell people how to do something are based on the coach's personal knowledge, intuition and experience of trying different methods with learners. This kind of experience is vital to good coaching because the 'how' to execute a skilled action is much more important than just stating what it looks like. And this is especially important when teaching dangerous or complicated movements (e.g., canoe rolling).

Another distinction can be made between direct and indirect verbal guidance. Direct verbal guidance refers to technique once again, but specifies something clear about the task in hand, e.g., "angle your chest to the side wall" or "point your toes". Indirect verbal guidance or 'hinting' as it is sometimes known is a technique for achieving a particular movement without exactly specifying it. For example, to encourage a novice skier to rotate the body towards the fall line, the instructor might tell the skier to imagine placing one hand in the opposite pocket. This has the effect of rotating the learner's trunk in the appropriate direction. In swimming, learners are told to imagine moving through a narrow tube. This helps to avoid exaggerated movements sideways and also inclining the body (see Figure 7). In teaching a support stroke in canoeing it is useful to tell the learner to pull the blade under the canoe — even though this never actually happens.

Similarly, to develop correct hip movement in a trampoline somersault, the learner would be told to push the hips through the ceiling window! In climbing, the novice is told to 'climb with your eyes'. And in many ball sports the learner is told to 'keep your eyes on the ball'. This not only provides useful flight information of course, but also helps to angle the body to the approaching ball in the correct manner. Comments such as these can be fruitful because they make it easier for the coach to describe complicated movements and also easier for the learner to identify with the coach's requirements. In the same way it is frequently useful to provide learners with rules or principles which help explain what they are doing and which may apply across a number of different sports (e.g., moving off the ball, anticipation, wide base of support, angular momentum). Evidence suggests that if people understand more fully what they are doing then they remember better. However, the teaching of strategic or mechanical principles needs to be dealt with in a sensitive manner and certainly with regard to the learner's intellectual level. Hinting is a coaching technique which can be applied with very good effect, but demands imagination from the coach and, of course, experience to discover what works best.

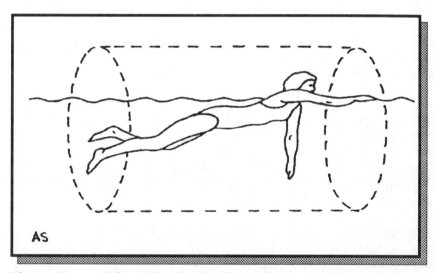

Figure 7:   **Schematic showing how a learner might visualise swimming within a constraining tube.**

An additional facet of verbal guidance is what Ormond (1992) calls 'prompting'. Ormond talks about giving the learner brief cues during performance (cues which may take the form of a single word or even a gesture) which are timed and designed to maximise the learner's attempt to perform correctly. Thus, rather than simply instructing and waiting for the learner to complete a movement, which may turn out incorrectly, the teacher/coach prompts during the movement in the hope of shaping it more correctly. This is a procedure which many good teachers do automatically.

Verbal guidance has been shown to be particularly beneficial with those activities where discrimination, decision-making and perceptual judgements are critical. It is simpler to talk about the intricacies of tactical and strategic play (backed up with demonstrations of course) — at least initially — than just demonstrating them in action without a verbal description. It seems that 'open' skills benefit more from verbal guidance than 'closed' skills. This makes sense when considering the broader scope and varied nature of open-skilled situations. It is also suggested by the research that verbal instruction has more meaning at higher levels of skill. The logic here would be that the more experienced a person, the greater is the skill vocabulary, so to speak, and hence the greater the profit from technical descriptions using the jargon of the sport.

To illustrate, the experienced badminton player will know what it means to 'shorten (or lengthen) the backswing' or 'keep a wide base and flexed knees', whereas the novice might be lost. This is not to conclude that learners should not be spoken to! The coach should acknowledge that the novice or learner may not have the same kind of attention span as the expert and certainly not the knowledge base required for understanding and that his/her goals are directed more towards 'having a go' than 'listening about it'. Research has shown that too much talk can have a detrimental effect on learners, and there is much anecdotal evidence to support this.

Are you the kind of instructor depicted in Figure 8? These comments suggest that there are weaknesses with verbal instruction.

Figure 8:
As a coach, do you like listening to your own voice?!

It is often assumed that instructions are readily understood by the learner. One should really be guarded because people — especially novices — do not always reveal their lack of understanding. Failure in practice may not be due to an inability to carry out the movements but a failure to fully understand the task. It should also be realised that the learner has to make a transition from the spoken word to a physical movement, in the same way required with visual demonstrations. With a verbal description however, the transition is less direct, requires more attention and also imposes an extra memory load on the learner. Finally, it should be borne in mind that the learner is probably eager to practise and hence an over-lengthy description may bore or frustrate the learner and even create unnecessary feelings of uncertainty.

Manual guidance

Having dealt with vision and hearing, it remains to examine the physical or kinesthetic sense and the importance of internal sensations in learning. Boyce (1991) makes out a case for teachers to spend less time on 'show and tell' procedures and more time on those which encourage the feel of movement. The feel of movement is very much associated with the kinesthetic sense which has for many years been of great scientific and practical interest to sports people — physical educationalists and coaches alike. In some ways it is the least understood of all our senses. Questions surrounding its exact nature — which nerve receptors serve kinesthesis and whether kinesthesis also includes our perception of touch and balance — permeate the academic literature (e.g., Sharp, 1971). Investigators have examined our capacity to remember kinesthetic information, the contribution that movement-generated feedback makes to our level of arousal (does chewing gum keep you alert?) and the relative importance it plays in maintaining balance (e.g., Lee & Lishman, 1975). One thing is clear. The kinesthetic sense is a potentially rich medium for guiding learners. Movement not only gives expression to the learner's endeavours but also provides a channel through which the coach can communicate.

Specifically, manual guidance involves some kind of physical contact between the learner and coach or between the learner and another device, e.g., a swimming float. As well as providing information about 'how to do it', a major intention of manual guidance is to control the movements made by the learner. Specifically, the aim is to minimise or eliminate completely the amount of error in the movement. The literature makes a distinction between two kinds of guidance: physical restriction and forced response (Holding, 1965). With physical restriction, the learner's movements are restricted either by another person or by an external object. Typical examples would be the use of a float in swimming or a waist belt in gymnastics. Here, the coach or device acts in a guiding capacity whilst the learner applies the effort to produce the action. Another example would be the use of a hinged plastic device which attaches to the tips of downhill skis. This device is frequently employed with physically disabled skiers who may have difficulty controlling their actions. The device is sufficiently flexible to provide 'give' when the skier is moving and will snap into two sections if the skier falls.

With forced response methods, a second person/s physically transports the learner through the movement with little or no effort from the learner. An example would be the coach moving a player's arm through a tennis serve action. Another would be a gymnastics coach transporting a young child through a rolling movement. These techniques reduce errors on the part of the learner and dramatically reduce the elements of fear and danger. In this way they help boost confidence and encourage learners into situations where they would otherwise not venture (e.g., deep water), and often allow skill progression well beyond previous levels. For these reasons it is considered that manual guidance is best used with very young children, older people (beyond middle age) and special groups such as those with low skill capacity or physical disabilities.

Despite the obvious advantages of manual guidance (e.g., consider the widespread use of floats in swimming) the research is somewhat guarded on the benefits. It is thought primarily that manual techniques assist in giving the learner ideas about the gross spatial patterns involved in movements (e.g., an up-side-down position in a somersault or a horizontal posture in water). They do not always help in the discovery of which cues to attend to or the forces involved in actions. For this reason, manual guidance is used more in sports which are closed in nature (e.g., gymnastics and trampolining) as opposed to open sports such as team games.

The essential problem with manual guidance is that the feeling of movement which it creates is not the same as the individual's own kinesthetic perception — the kinesthetic sense responds differently. Thus if the coach moves a learner's arm through a serving action it will not result in the same 'feeling' as if the learner had initiated the movement. The pay-off is that the guided action is technically correct. It seems clear that physical restriction produces a more realistic picture than forced response, but the weakness remains that the learner does not receive exactly the correct kind of feedback and may even be encouraged to depend on the support given. It is also worth mentioning that current theories of learning emphasise the critical nature of active participation by the learner which is negated to an extent by the use of manual techniques. This particular topic will be addressed in a later chapter.

The learning gradient

Some of the ideas expressed in this chapter have been used by Priest & Hammerman (1989) to formulate what they call the learning gradient and this is a useful concept with which to finish. They suggest that four stages to teaching an activity: speaking to the learner, demonstrating the activity, ensuring the learner practises the activity and questioning the learner about the activity, can be placed on a continuum of 'amount learned' (see Figure 9).

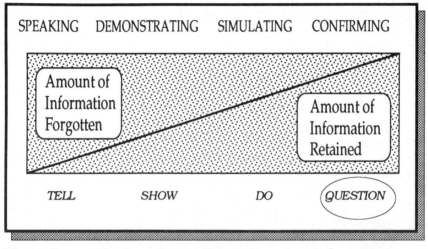

SPEAKING   DEMONSTRATING   SIMULATING   CONFIRMING

Amount of Information Forgotten

Amount of Information Retained

TELL   SHOW   DO   (QUESTION)

Figure 9: **The 'learning gradient' shows how information forgotten/retained by the learner relates to the method of instructional input.**

In this scheme, *telling the learner* imparts little information, as most is lost or forgotten. *Showing what to do* is better ('a picture paints a thousand words'). To learn, one must practise to correctly perform skills and fully understand their uses. However, not until learners have been finally questioned on their knowledge, their ability to analyse and assess, and their skill in evaluation, judging, predicting, etc. can the coach or teacher be fully sure that information has been retained. Priest & Hammerman (1989) put great store in the fourth of these components. Readers may wish to examine the extent to which their own practices employ this principle!

Summary

1. Guidance is information provided by the coach before the learner makes an attempt at the movement.
2. Practice is the act of going through a movement without any guidance whilst training is the process of learning with guidance.
3. Practice is potentially limited in a number of ways:
   a. trial and error may result in the formation of bad habits;
   b. extra time is required to eradicate bad habits;
   c. the learner's performance level remains low;
   d. risk of dropout from the sport is increased.

4.   Guidance is provided through the three senses — vision, audition and kinesthesis.

5.   The separate senses can each provide the same information and they interact to give the learner a total picture of the movement or task.

6.   Visual guidance can be one of three kinds: demonstrations provided by the coach, expert or learner; visual materials such as film loops or wallcharts; changes to the display such as the addition of a sight screen or colouring important pieces of apparatus to cue on.

7.   Demonstrations rely on learning by imitation; they are intuitively appealing; they are immediate and practical to employ; they avoid lengthy verbal descriptions; they should be used with caution, i.e., they should be relevant, accurate and repeated. The position of the learner must be considered and the time spent on demonstrations should be balanced against total practice time.

8.   Visual aids which are static in nature are of questionable value.

9.   Video film of experts/learners has a number of advantages. It is intuitively appealing, offers immediate feedback and replay/slow motion facility.

10.   Video is effective only if certain conditions are met. The learner's attention must be directed to specific points. Practice must be allowed immediately following replay and the learner must have the potential to copy the points made on the video. Repeated viewing is vital to success and the learner must be motivated to succeed.

11.   Rearranging apparatus or highlighting features by colouring/texturing is a useful way of emphasising important cues.

12.   Verbal instructions serve two purposes: to describe what an action looks like and to explain how it may be executed.

13.   Direct verbal guidance expresses something concrete about an action or task, whereas indirect instruction hints at the action or indicates another action which if attempted results in the desired one.

14.   Verbal guidance seems to be particularly useful for advanced learners and with skills that have an important 'perceptual' element, e.g., tactical/strategic play in soccer.

15.   Verbal guidance is limited in a number of ways. The learner may not understand. The learner is required to 'cross the bridge' between words and action. The learner may be bored by lengthy talks and there exists the difficulty of explaining some movements in words.

16.   Manual guidance takes two forms:
      a.   physical restriction where a second person or other device is used to guide the learner through a movement
      b.   forced response where a second person physically transports the learner through a movement

17. Manual guidance is valuable in:
    a. reducing the fear element in difficult/dangerous activities.
    b. reducing the element of danger;
    c. highlighting spatial elements in a movement;
    d. illustrating an action which would be difficult to express in words;
    e. use with special groups, e.g., young children, old people, those with low skill levels.
18. Manual guidance is limited because it provides different feedback from normal performance and reduces the learner's degree of active participation.

Discussion questions

1. What are your views about novices practising by themselves? For example, do you think it is good for the novice to make errors during learning?
2. Can you think of an example in your sport where once a bad habit has formed it is difficult to eliminate?
3. Why does the habit appear in the first place?
4. Examine a situation in your sport where you could communicate the idea of a skill using different senses.
5. Is it likely that you would use different senses to get across the message?
6. Have you ever examined whether your own personal demonstrations are correct?
7. How useful is it to strike a balance between your own demonstrations and those of, say, a team member?
8. At what stage/s in the learner's progress do you think demonstrations are most important?
9. In your sport is it important to consider how people are positioned with respect to a demonstration?
10. Comment on the view that the practical difficulties in using video (e.g., cost, operational skills) outweigh the benefits.
11. If you have used video in your sport state the circumstances in which its use has been most valuable.
12. Are there instances in your sport where visual cues are highlighted in some way to make it easier for the learner or expert performer? If so, state what they are.
13. In your coaching or teaching are you aware of the important distinction between describing and explaining skill?
14. Consider an activity or movement in your sport and write down the instructions you would use to express HOW to do it.
15. How do you tell whether people have understood your instructions?
16. At what stage/s of learning do you think that 'chat' is most beneficial?

17. Can you provide examples of manual guidance as used in your sport?
18. Are there particular instances when manual guidance is of special value in your sport?
19. What are the major problems with manual guidance?

References

Bandura, A. (1969) *Principles of behaviour modification.* New York: Holt, Reinhart & Winston.

Barclay, C.D., Cutting, J.E. and Kozlowski, L.T. (1978) Temporal spatial factors in gait perception that influence gender recognition. *Perception & Psychophysics*, **23**, 145–152.

Boyce, B.A. (1991) Beyond show and tell — teaching the feel of the movement. *The Journal of Physical Education, Recreation and Dance*, **62**, 1, 18–20.

Harrison, J.M., and Blakemore, C. (1989) *Instructional Strategies for Physical Education.* Dubuque, IA: W. C. Brown.

Hickey, K. Quoted in Sharp, R.H. (1986) *Acquiring skill — Coach Education Modules.* Edinburgh: The Scottish Sports Council.

Holding, D.H. (1965) *Principles of training.* London: Pergamon Press.

Jameson, J. Quoted in Sharp, R.H. (1986) *Acquiring skill — Coach Education Modules.* Edinburgh: The Scottish Sports Council.

Kerwin, D.S. and Sprunt, K.E. (1988) Energy patterns in gymnastic upstarts. In *Proceedings of the Annual Conference of The British Association of Sports Science*, Exeter, September.

Lee, D.N. and Lishman, R. (1975) Vision in movement and balance. *New Scientist*, January, 59–61, 1975.

Newell, K.M., Morris, L.R. and Scully, D.M. (1985) Augmented information and the acquisition of skill in physical activity. In R.L. Terjung (Ed.), *Exercise and Sport Sciences Review* (Vol 13). New York: Macmillan.

Ormond, T.C. (1992) The prompt/feedback package in physical education. *Journal of Physical Education, Recreation and Dance*, **63**, 1, 64–67.

Priest, S. and Hammerman, D. (1989) Teaching outdoor adventure skills. *Adventure Education*, **6**, 4, 16–18, 1989.

Scully, D.M. (1988) Visual perception of human movement: The use of demonstrations in teaching motor skills. *British Journal of Physical Education (Research Supplement)*, **19**, 12–14.

Shedden, J. Quoted in Sharp, R.H. (1986) *Acquiring skill — Coach Education Modules.* Edinburgh: The Scottish Sports Council.

Thorndike, E.L. (1927) The law of effect. *American Journal of Psychology*, **39**, 212–222.

Chapter 4

PROVISION OF FEEDBACK

Introduction

Feedback is a word which is used to express many things, e.g., reinforcement, reward, knowledge of results and so on. It is taken to mean information which occurs as a result of executing a movement. It is considered by many people to be the single-most important variable in the learning process.

A useful start is to take a close look at what we mean by feedback. One good reason for examining the word closely is because it is borrowed from disciplines quite different from the world of coaching and teaching. The word comes from the field of control engineering. It refers specifically to the flow of information within a control system to inform the system what it is doing and what effect its constituent parts are having on one another. An example of a control system which contains a feedback device (sometimes called a servomechanism) is a home refrigerator. A refrigerator aims to keep its contents cool, but only down to a prescribed temperature. If the level goes lower than that set by the owner, the fridge switches itself off and consequently proceeds to warm up. When the preset temperature is exceeded the fridge is switched on again to begin the process of cooling once more. The feedback in this example is the present air temperature within the refrigerator. Figure 10 illustrates this schematically in relation to a domestic central heating system.

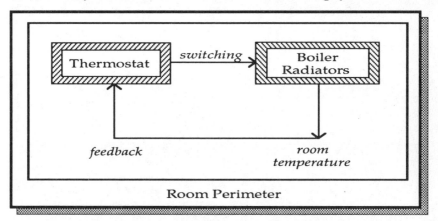

Figure 10: An example of a feedback system. In this example, feedback is always the current room temperature. The thermostat monitors the air temperature and switches the boiler on/off depending on whether the thermostat's pre-set temperature is exceeded.

It will be recognised that for feedback information to be of any use, the fridge or heating system must have a means of sensing the information. The sensing device in both cases is the thermostat which opens and closes an electrical circuit as appropriate. Any system which uses feedback must have a sensing element.

It is relevant to point out that there are two basic kinds of control systems. A control system which can monitor the effects of its own operation is called a 'closed-loop' system. Refrigerators and central heating systems operate like this. In contrast, an 'open-loop' system does not have a feedback device. An example is an ordinary electrical bar fire. A bar fire when switched on will continue to heat the room regardless of its effect. Figure 11 shows these two systems in schematic form.

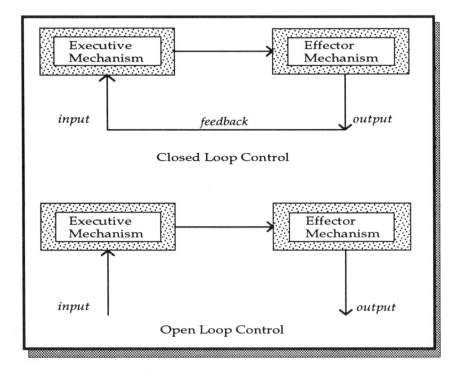

Figure 11: In both parts of the figure the executive mechanism is that part of the system which issues commands (e.g., a thermostat). The effector system carries out those commands (e.g., a boiler). With a closed-loop system the executive mechanism is able to 'sense' the output from the effector mechanism. With an open-loop system this avenue of communication absent.

The executive mechanism is that component which issues the commands, (e.g., the switch on the bar fire), whilst the effector mechanism actually carries out the commands (e.g., the heating element). There are many situations in everyday life which can be examined in this manner. Take for example a typical industrial concern which comprises management and workforce. Management could take an autocratic stance and not listen to its workforce (open loop) or it could adopt a democratic stance by listening to its workers and making changes based on information received a (closed loop). Another example would be the reader's own coaching or teaching style. Sometimes it might be appropriate to make decisions based on experience without consulting the group or individual learner; on other occasions (perhaps most frequently) it is better to listen to learners so that coaching becomes a two-way affair. Which style is better? It is likely that in both examples, sometimes an open-loop approach is better whilst at other times a closed-loop approach is preferable.

Systems which employ feedback are more sophisticated and adaptable than those which do not. For this reason, the use of feedback as a guiding tool is central to good coaching and teaching . From the learner's point of view, in order to move skilfully, to learn and adapt to an ever-changing world there is a need to constantly observe actions, their effect and react accordingly. Feedback is critical to learning and to successful performance. A simple demonstration of the importance of feedback is seen in the act of picking up a cup from a table. An initial command from the brain results in the arm extending in the cup's direction. As the arm moves closer, the eyes make an accurate assessment of distance between cup and hand (use of visual feedback) which allows the hand to move more precisely for the fine grasping action. Visual feedback may be used once or twice in such a task.

The examples just given illustrate a number of features which are of value in any discussion of skill acquisition. Firstly, for feedback information to be of any value there must be some kind of model against which it is compared. In the fridge example the reference is the preset temperature. Secondly, the system must be able to detect the error between the reference and the feedback and consequently do something useful about it, i.e., effect some kind of corrective action to minimise the error. Thirdly, it must be noted that feedback is, in effect, information which tells the system about errors produced, i.e., how far away from the intended performance is actual performance. Feedback information derives from the difference between desired and actual performance. From the point of view of the learner and the coach this poses a potential problem in that such information must be presented to the performer in a manner which has a positive influence on learning. As we all know, it is very easy to find fault and criticise — even naive observers are sometimes good at spotting performance errors. The real skill is in turning such information into positive assistance so that it is used to motivate people to improvements and not turn them away. We shall pick up these issues later following a broader look at what feedback means for human learning and performance and what effect it has on the individual. To place this discussion into the correct context, it's useful to note the views of a practising coach (Crisfield, quoted in Sharp, 1986).

> Feedback is absolutely vital. Lacrosse is a very complex game because there are 24 people on the field of play. Consequently, decision making has to involve almost all those people. Therefore it's very difficult to evaluate your own role without some kind of external feedback. I try to give them two forms of feedback — objective feedback from game analysis as well as subjective feedback from my own perceptions. I try to give players feedback on a personal basis, face to face, and if that's not possible, which sometimes in a large team game it isn't, I'm forced to give them feedback on paper. I try and give feedback as soon as possible after the game but this depends on the individual and what has happened in the game.

Let us now look at some of the research findings which support this kind of thinking. It appears that we use feedback of different kinds constantly, simply to regulate and control moment to moment activity. This is particularly so with physiological systems such as breathing and bodily temperature which are maintained at an adequate level despite a constantly changing environment (the process of homeostasis). It would seem that internal feedback systems take care of all these things quite automatically. The value of feedback in controlling physical activity is demonstrated by those studies which artificially remove or distort feedback. In one study, county level squash players were asked to play whilst wearing headphones through which was played 'white noise'. The noise was chosen to mask any sound of contact between ball, racquet and the walls. In many cases players found it very difficult to time their strokes effectively and were very surprised at their failure. They were still able to make contact with the ball, but their timing accuracy deteriorated markedly. In another study people were asked to balance standing on a narrow lathe of wood whilst the room was physically swayed a minute amount backwards and forwards. Invariably, people found it more difficult to balance when the room moved compared to when it was stationary. What do these studies reveal? Well, not only do they demonstrate the importance of feedback, but they indicate that feedback control can operate quite automatically without any conscious awareness of the information being used to control behaviour. The squash players were not aware they used auditory cues and the subjects in the balance experiment were not conscious of using visual cues to help balance. The studies also indicate that different sources of feedback (i.e., auditory and visual) are used in controlling physical activity. One generalisation from the research literature is that through learning people change from a predominantly visual/verbal method of feedback control to one where they rely more on internal or kinesthetic feedback. This was the view expressed by Fitts (Fitts & Posner, 1967) and detailed in the first chapter. The squash and balance studies show further that experts do not just rely on internal feedback, but use a number of different kinds of information — which may depend on the kind of task in hand.

Let us now examine some of the major principles of feedback which apply to the study of skill learning. These principles stem from a number of sources — the experience of coaches and teachers, research findings, as well as theoretical principles.

Effects of feedback

Firstly, let us consider the proposed effect of feedback on learning. It has been suggested that although feedback provides information about performance it may serve three different purposes — to motivate learners, to change performance and to reinforce learning. In its role as a motivator, feedback tells the learner that errors are being reduced and consequently that skill level is increasing. In this respect feedback acts rather like a reward. It is well known that people are motivated to improve if suitably rewarded and are stimulated to greater efforts if they succeed (the so-called 'law of effect' — see Chapter 1) but, sometimes caution must be expressed when providing feedback. The coach needs to be careful because with some learners, 'error' information in the form of say a comment about what went wrong, may inhibit learning as the comment is construed as criticism. The point was made before that feedback must be presented in a constructive manner if it is to have a positive effect. The coach must therefore consider the manner in which feedback is provided, the timing as well as the kind and amount of feedback given. Sensitivity to the learner's personality, needs and goals and intellectual capacity should provide answers to these problems.

The second and perhaps most common function of feedback is to provide information about performance. If a ski instructor tells the learner that body weight is too far backwards, the learner uses this information to adjust posture to a more forward position. Information feedback such as this only 'works' if the learner can interpret the feedback and judge it against a reference or model of what is correct. In the ski example, the instructor might ask the learner to lean forwards and then backwards to compare the correct and incorrect positions. The coach might then augment this by demonstrating the incorrect and correct positions for the learner to see. Feedback might not always be so clearly interpreted however, especially in sports where visual feedback is absent. Consider a front drop in trampolining where clearly the lower legs cannot be seen by the performer. It is virtually impossible for the novice to gauge leg position because kinesthetic sensitivity of the knee joint is very crude.

Therefore, telling the learner about incorrect leg position may be less informative than physically moving the legs into and out of the correct position several times. In its informative role, feedback narrows down the discrepancy between what the coach and learner are trying to achieve and what the learner is presently doing. This process hinges on correct error identification and the establishment of a model of excellence.

The final function of feedback is a reinforcing one. It confirms with the learner that progress is being made or that the same error is still being committed or that performance is accurate. Confirmation may be just as desirable as new information. Generally, coaches and teachers alike tend to ignore the value of confirmation because the assumption is made that learners who perform correctly know they are doing so. This is not always the case!

As a rule, all three aspects may combine and it may not matter where the focus lies. Sometimes however, the coach may wish to direct feedback for a particular purpose, as when willing a person to greater effort following, say, an injury or loss of confidence. In this case the coach's comments — which may not accurately reflect the learner's performance — are intended as a spur to effort, to enhance confidence and develop interest.

Models

The second topic to consider is the one of models mentioned before. The provision and utilisation of feedback assumes that the coach has a reference or standard by which to judge performance. Feedback cannot be evaluated without a definitive model for comparison which is technically appropriate. A clear example of this is seen in those sports where successful performance depends largely on conformity to a prescribed movement pattern, e.g., trampolining or high jumping. A coach teaching the Fosbury flop say, must have a clear idea in his/her mind's eye about correct technique to be able to judge incorrect attempts at the movement. Such a model must be valid in meeting all the relevant criteria (e.g., mechanical laws) but also flexible in the sense that it allows for individual variations (because of say body type) and different levels of performance. The model for, say, a beginner (for example, a front somersault in trampolining) would be quite different from that for the expert. The sensitive coach therefore assesses feedback in relationship to a flexible model dependent on both the individual and present stage of success.

A further requirement of the coach is the ability to detect differences between the model and the learner's performance. The ability to spot errors will depend on an in-depth knowledge of the activity. Such knowledge may arise from personal participation in the sport and experience of watching and coaching people at different skill levels. It may also arise from more sophisticated examinations based on video film or computerised player analysis and it may include information about the physiological and biomechanical requirements of the activity. Armed with such knowledge the coach will know that technical weaknesses are not necessarily learning problems *per se*. Poor technique may lie in say a fitness deficiency or possibly a weakness caused by injury. In swimming, for example, a common problem is that learners tend to sink their hips too low. This happens because the head is held too high out of the water. The actual problem however, may result because the learner has not developed correct breathing. In this case the coach would take the swimmer back to basic confidence work, helping him or her to swim with face submerged.

Error-spotting is often difficult because performance is too rapid for considered appraisal. This is an area where video replay comes into its own. A related skill is the need for the coach to rectify the errors once spotted. Feedback is therefore only the start of a complex process in which the coach compares a learner's skill with an ideal model, evaluates feedback and then guides the learner through some kind of corrective practice.

It may be worth highlighting at this point the important difference between what is known in the literature as knowledge of results (KR) and knowledge of performance (KP). A coach may provide the learner with information pertaining to the outcome of performance (e.g., the ball landed in the rough, or the time taken was 12 sec.) — this is KR — or he/she may discuss details of the movement itself (e.g., the gymnastic routine was clumsy, or knee-rise in the sprint was too low) — KP. It seems logical that feedback in the form of KR is more appropriate to open skills (because success is measured largely by outcomes) and KP more appropriate in closed skills (where success is monitored largely through movement execution). The limitation here however, is to over-simplify the two categories of skill. For example, closed activities such as diving or sports acrobatics involve more than the execution of a well co-ordinated sequence of movements and similarly, skill in sports which are predominantly open in nature such as soccer, embody more than the capacity to reach tangible targets such as score goals.

A better way of assessing the right kind of feedback is to adopt a 'systems approach' (see Figure 12, overleaf) and look at all sports in the same way. This approach focuses the coach's attention firstly on perception and questions whether the learner has a perceptual problem which requires examination. It then proceeds with decision making and finally technique. In this way the chances of spotting errors and providing the right kind of feedback are maximised.

Before leaving the subject of models, it should be underlined that current opinion also argues the learner too, should develop a model or 'motor plan' of what is required. It makes sense that the learner should play an active role in his or her own learning — a point which is picked up in the next chapter. It is argued this not only raises motivation but also makes feedback more meaningful later in practice. It also helps to make the learner a more informed participant in the learning process. One problem is that because the learner's model is internal in nature, there is little way of knowing if he or she is formulating an accurate model or even attempting to do so. Ways of examining both of these problems are looked at in the next chapter.

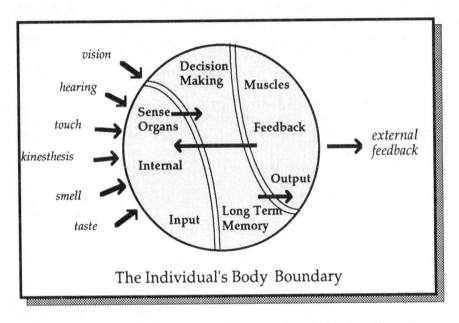

The Individual's Body Boundary

Figure 12: **A systems approach to human behaviour based on the model of Shedden (1982).**

Forms of feedback

Feedback can take on a number of forms. For example, feedback can occur as a natural consequence of the activity (e.g., sight of the ball hitting the cross bar following an attempt at goal) or it may be augmented information such as the coach's remarks or a press photograph. Feedback can also be categorised with regard to the various senses. It may be visual, auditory or kinesthetic in nature. The coach should consider how these various categories may be used for the research suggests that people use different kinds of feedback at different times and in different situations. Some individuals are able to self-analyse and require minimal prompting whilst those less confident may benefit from constant encouragement and advice. The sport or activity in question is also important. For example, in closed actions where consistency of movement is important the coach may wish to emphasise feedback which directs the learner to his/her bodily positions and movements. Encouraging the learner to think about the 'feel' of movement or employing manual techniques of guidance may be important. In open skills where skill reflects how well the person reacts to a constantly changing environment (as in badminton say), feedback which relates the players' actions to their consequences might be more important. In badminton, forcing the learner to focus on the shuttle's direction in relation to the action which produced it, either at the time of playing or later on video, might be most beneficial. With more skilled players it may not be necessary for the coach to provide augmented or supplementary feedback because the learner can assess internal feedback. Good coaches would expect to develop this ability in their athletes.

Stage of learning may also be important in dictating the kind of feedback which is most relevant. Some research evidence shows that beginners tend to rely heavily on visual/verbal sources of input and only later in learning utilise internal or kinesthetic information (see Fitts, Chapter 1). If this is the case, then, in early learning, talking about problems and illustrating them through video should be effective. Later in learning, when the learner has established a skill model and 'ironed out' most errors it would make sense to encourage him/her to introspect on performance and develop a sensitivity to the 'feel' of movement. However, a word of caution at this point for it would be unwise to think this sequence always applies (remember the expert squash players who used auditory feedback). It is also clear from the literature that individuals choose to select information which appeals to them. There is no reason therefore to assume that, say, video feedback or kinesthetic feedback aren't useful at all levels of learning — but only for some people.

Video has been mentioned a number of times so far, but it should not be assumed that it is the panacea for all problems. Chapter 3 examined the conditions which must apply if it is to be of any value.

Timing of feedback

Let us now examine some of the temporal aspects of feedback administration. There is an important distinction between intrinsic and external (or extrinsic) feedback. Intrinsic feedback is ever present and is a natural consequence of movement. It occurs either at the time of execution (e.g., when a cyclist feels pain in legs during an uphill sprint), or on termination (e.g., when the basketball player sees the ball enter the ring). External feedback is not an automatic consequence of movement and may not be present. It is additional to intrinsic feedback and may be administered by a coach or teacher during or following the learner's performance.

Feedback, by definition, is always received by the individual a short period after action. In mechanical systems this is seen in the manner in which they always react a little later than desired (e.g., turbo systems in motor car engines, central heating thermostats). The same follows in human behaviour. For example, a novice rugby player who slices a kick to touch may have to wait and see where the ball is going before deciding what to do. The expert will recognise errors much sooner and chase the ball earlier, but in both cases there is a finite time lag (caused through nervous transmission, decision making, etc.) between action and reaction. Feedback delay cannot be avoided, but it can be minimised through anticipation: i.e., the player can make a guess about what is to happen (as when the sprinter anticipates the gun) which enables him/her to react on time — albeit with the attendant possibility of error. Leaving aside anticipation for the time being (Chapter 6 deals with this topic), it is important to note that feedback and time are inextricably bound together.

An important question which refers to external feedback is 'When should the coach provide feedback?'. Research seems to indicate that the sooner after performance feedback is given, the less likely the learner will forget what the feedback pertains to and the less likely he/she will practice incorrect movements. Marshall (quoted in Sharp, 1986) expresses this very well:

> When a skill is being performed it is important to give feedback at certain points, firstly because people don't know when the faults are coming in and secondly because you can perhaps encourage them to correct faults by giving them the right instruction. At the end of the performance try to give the feedback as soon as they come off the trampoline. It is important that you remember what you've just done because if you wait even a minute the performer will lose the feeling of what he has been doing and it will be more difficult to relate to what the coach is saying.

Immediate feedback therefore seems to be the ideal approach. However, unlike the trampolining example just given, this may not always be practical (e.g., if the coach is on the sideline during a match). Also, it may not always be desirable. It could be confusing to the learner to comment on performance (say an attempt at a new gymnastic vault) the very moment it finishes. A few seconds should be given to recover from and reflect on the performance — perhaps to evaluate internal feedback first — before the coach offers advice. A general guide for the coach would be to 'count to ten' before giving feedback.

Further evidence from the research literature shows that as well as delay of feedback, the time interval lapsing before the learner has a next attempt at the skill is also critical. If practice following the coach's advice is delayed (or perhaps not allowed) then the learner forgets the advice and is unable to relate it to a renewed attempt at the skill. The exact time interval between practices will, of course, depend on many practical factors (e.g., how fatigued the person is or how many other people are involved in the practice) but, it should certainly not exceed a matter of minutes. Hickey, a boxing coach (quoted in Sharp, 1986), discusses the matter of feedback delay and suggests that a critical issue is whether the individual is receptive to feedback:

In training it is important to give the feedback immediately and to make it as positive as possible. Depending upon the complexity of the skill being learned it would then be up to the coach to decide how the individual should be approached in terms of his own personality and his own requirements, but also the type of fault that was appearing. When it comes to competition there is another factor which is the actual ability of the individual boxer to be receptive to comments made. To try to give the feedback too close to the contest may be pointless. When you give feedback to a boxer after a contest is important. To give a general indication in terms of how well he's done is sufficient when his mind may be in a turmoil — he's on a high if he's won or a low if he's lost. If one went into too positive an analysis of his performance then it would not be well received. The balance of the emotional feelings of the boxer should determine to the coach by experience at what point the feedback would be received and applied to future performance.

A further question which centres on the topic of time is how often should feedback be given? Both anecdotal evidence and recent research suggests that giving information following every attempt does not necessarily produce the best learning effect. Accumulating feedback over a number of trials and emphasising what appears to be the important aspects seems to be better because it provides more reliable information and also allows the learner to concentrate longer on internal feedback sources.

Amount and precision of feedback

Finally, let us examine the amount and precision of feedback which should be given. Firstly the amount of feedback. By and large, coaches and teachers alike, perhaps because of their vast fund of technical knowledge are apt to give too much information to the learner. They watch a performance, spot errors and then risk bamboozling the learner by examining all the things that need to be corrected. This is a difficult situation for the coach. What he/she should do is weigh up the most important issues, select one or two and then present them in a simple and precise manner. It may well be that correcting one error has a knock-on effect in solving a number of others. This might be the case with the novice skier whose major problem often is one of weight distribution. Correcting this often allows the skis to run together better, creates better control of speed and also allows for more efficient turning. The instructor may not even need to draw attention to these problems because they are automatically solved through attention to a more fundamental one.

There is sometimes a case for reducing feedback by physically excluding certain sources. Some types of feedback may have a detrimental effect on the learner, e.g., comments from fellow learners. In such cases it would be wise to say arrange practice in isolation from other people. Also, some kinds of feedback, by virtue of their very presence may divert attention away from more important sources of feedback. In putting (golf) for example, it has been known for learners to be blindfolded to encourage attention to the physical movement and away from the actual outcome of the stroke. Similarly, novice skiers learning to snow-plough can be directed to close their eyes which helps them focus more on what the legs should be doing (pushing the knees forwards and the heels outwards) and less on what the skis are doing. And in canoeing, it sometimes helps when practising a ferry-glide to close the eyes which helps concentration on the effect of paddling actions. Such techniques may appear a little dramatic, but (under the appropriate conditions) they add to the variety of the coach's repertoire and may allow him/her to solve infrequent, but perhaps persistent problems which other methods cannot tackle.

Turning now to the topic of feedback precision, it is known that the precision or detail of feedback depends not only on how refined skill needs to be, but also the intellectual capacity and stage of learning of the person. Advice couched in simple terms and certainly with a positive emphasis on praise — perhaps via a video recording — would be appropriate to the novice whereas a hard-hitting, but constructive technical account might suit the expert. Research evidence shows that the more detailed the feedback, the better the progress to the final goal. A good strategy therefore would be to err on the side of detail and then check — by questioning the learner and by watching carefully his/her subsequent attempts at the skill — to see if there has been understanding. Good coaches not only provide clear informative instructions, but also wait to observe whether their advice has been absorbed.

Another aspect about feedback precision which should be raised here concerns the extent to which the learner can actually use detailed information to improve actions. The results of an experiment by Fazey and Ramsey (1988) serve to illustrate this point. In a simple, repetitive finger-tapping task, subjects were asked to keep time with a metronome set at a given rate. When the pace was altered by a small amount they were able to adjust their actions automatically even though the increase in pace was not perceived. When however, they were asked by the experimenter to adjust the pace to a higher/lower rate, the smallest increment they could manage was much larger. It seems that the 'grain of control' or precision which the individual can apply following the use of verbal information is far coarser than that of lower-level 'automatic' systems. This suggests that the learner may not be able to utilise information provided by the coach if it requires a very fine change in performance. Again, this reinforces a point made before about the value of verbal feedback in learning. It seems that verbal feedback is most useful in orienting behaviour at a time when gross improvements are being made. In other words, it plays an important guidance role early in learning or when skill has broken down. Later in learning however, when most actions are controlled automatically, verbal feedback is of lesser value than the individual's internal analysis and rehearsal of what is being done.

Summary

1. Feedback is a source of information which arrives during or following a movement and which tells the person about the outcome of that movement.
2. We may not always be aware that we are using feedback to adjust on-going activity.
3. Feedback can arrive through different senses, e.g., vision, hearing.
4. The type of feedback used may depend on the nature of the sport or activity as well as the stage of learning.
5. For feedback to be of any value it must be compared against a reference or model (e.g., an athlete's previous performance).
6. Feedback is error information (sometimes called negative feedback). Both the coach and learner must use such information so that it acts in a positive manner to aid the learner.
7. Feedback can serve three purposes — to motivate, to change performance and to reinforce learning.
8. Feedback assumes the coach and learner have a model of what is correct.
9. The coach must be skilled not only in detecting the differences between feedback and the model, but also in planning subsequent practices.
10. It is important the coach is aware of how he/she manipulates the various kinds of feedback — internal/external, visual/auditory/kinesthetic.
11. Feedback is most effective when given shortly after performance. Subsequent practice must not be delayed or else the learner forgets what changes to make.
12. The more precise the feedback, the more beneficial its effect. The learner must be able to understand the feedback.

Discussion questions

1. How important is it to encourage the learner to identify his/her own faults with perhaps just confirmation from the coach?
2. When coaching do you adopt different 'standards' (models) for

different people dependent on say how tall or muscular they are?

3. Do you encounter problems in error -spotting? If so state what are the problems and how you deal with them.

4. Comment on the notion of allowing learners to make errors. Is this a desirable process?

5. In your sport, state how you would use the three senses (vision, audition, kinesthesis) to provide feedback.

6. Do you agree with the research that through learning people change from using visual feedback to using internal feedback?

7. How soon in the learning process do learners begin to feel what is correct without having to see or be told?

8. Are you aware of how quickly you tell the learner what is wrong?

9. Do you give the learner time to think about his/her attempts before making your case?

10. Do you think that sometimes you confuse the learner with your advice? Do you talk too much!?

11. Do you adjust the detail/difficulty of feedback with regard to individual performers?

12. Write down two examples of control systems found in everyday life, one of which is closed and the other open.

13. In the closed system identified, is there a period of time before feedback has an effect in changing the system? If so, are there any disadvantages in this delay?

14. Give an example of a bodily function which relies on feedback (e.g., breathing).

15. In the last question state:
    a. What dictates the 'normal' level of operation?
    b. What exactly constitutes the feedback?
    c. What changes actually take place, because of the feedback?

16. Give an example of an everyday activity, e.g., sitting down, in which feedback is used.

17. Can you think of a sporting skill which doesn't apparently require feedback for it to be controlled?

18. What techniques do you use to help learners acquire their own models or plans of action for a new skill?

19. Imagine a situation where one of your players has made an error, e.g., landed on the back following an attempted gymnastic action. How you would translate this error into constructive, positive feedback?

References

Crisfield, P. (1986) Quoted in Sharp, R.H. *Acquiring skill.* Coach Education Modules. Edinburgh: Scottish Sports Council.

Fazey, J. and Ramsey, I. (1988) Paper presented at the Annual Conference of the British Association of Sports Sciences, Exeter, September.

Fitts, P.M. and Posner, M.I. (1967) *Human performance.* Belmont, California: Brooks/Cole Publishing.

Hickey, K. (1986) Quoted in Sharp, R.H. *Acquiring skill.* Coach Education Modules. Edinburgh: Scottish Sports Council.

Marshall, P. (1986) Quoted in Sharp, R.H. *Acquiring skill.* Coach Education Modules. Edinburgh: Scottish Sports Council.

Shedden, J. (1982) *Skilful Skiing.* Wakefield: EP.

Chapter 5

PRACTICE MAKES PERFECT!

The last two chapters examined guidance — how we give information to the learner — and feedback — information which results from practice. Now we shall look at practice, itself a subject covering many different topics. This chapter will consider the role of making errors in learning, how skills should be broken down into smaller parts, how much time should be devoted to practice, as well as topics like mental practice and the management of practice.

Teaching and learning models

Often, the most obvious or logical things go unnoticed. In planning a practice session it makes sense to look at what has been done before by the learner and to consider how he/she should change as a result of the session. The reader might question how often detailed questions like this are considered. Knowing what has happened in the past and what is expected in the future makes it much easier to plan the nature of current practice. Psychologists refer to the outside elements as 'entry and terminal behaviours' and this scheme of things is depicted in Figure 13. It is one example of what was referred to before as a systems analysis — the process of breaking complicated problems down into logical, manageable sections. Notice that this approach is cyclical in nature where assessment and feedback are used to modify/plan for practice the next time around.

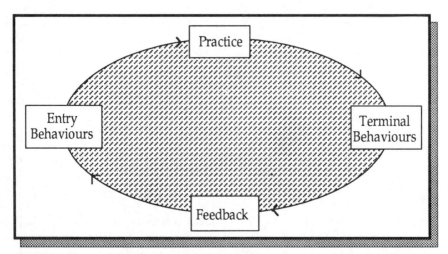

Figure 13: Learning can be thought of as a change between entry behaviour and terminal behaviour, mediated by practice and feedback.

Entry behaviours underpin the skills and knowledge which the learner possesses before he/she engages in practice. If the coach knows what these are (and most of the time the coach should be fully aware if working with the same people) then he/she is better able to plan events in a logical and smooth manner to ensure progression from the very start. The coach or teacher who doesn't bother or who hasn't checked the previous experience of say a newcomer, runs the risk of losing the learners' confidence and interest. To provide an example of this, consider a ski instructor faced with a new group of students on their first day. The good instructor will check safety matters such as clothing and bindings, but will also examine the experience of each individual. With this information to hand, the day can be planned accordingly. The instructor may decide to stay low down on the hill where the terrain is relatively gentle, or decide to treat the group as two different ability groups, and so on. At the very start the instructor is able to predict the likely outcome of the day in terms of skill progression and plan accordingly to make decisions about what the group is likely to achieve (the terminal behaviours).

Experience of working with different groups in the past will come in very handy here of course. Thus, acquiring basic information about learners to begin with and then using experience to judge the amount and kind of learning possible, the coach can begin to plan specific practice in a meaningful manner. This particular approach could be applied to any sport and is very general in nature, but there are numerous others methods. Typical of many is one devised by Pease (1977).

Pease adopts the view that the teaching process should mirror the learning process, i.e., the stages involved in planning and organising practice should be based on the phases through which the learner passes as he/she becomes more proficient. This scheme of things is described in Table 1 and is now elaborated.

Table 1: **A simplified learning/teaching model. Adapted from Pease (1977).**

The Learner	The Teacher/Coach
1. Perceive and desire goal	1. Provide 'set to learn'; provide a model of the goal
2. Identify relevant stimuli	2. Provide teaching cues
3. Formulate motor plan	3. Assist learners with motor plan formation
4. Emit a response	4. Provide learners with opportunity to practise
5. Attend to results	5. Provide learning cues and assist learners in interpreting results — and
6. Revise motor plan	6. Adjust their performances

A model of learning

The left-hand side of Table 1 lists the learning stages and is taken from an earlier report by Gentile (1972). The right-hand side is meant to mirror these stages. Let us look initially at Gentile's ideas on how people learn and the seven stages she identifies. Initially, she says that learners must be motivated to learn and must possess an idea about what to do. It is well known of course that people learn best only if they want to improve. Understanding why a new skill is important however, is not always obvious to the learner, especially if practice does not have a clear relationship to the final skill or game in question. Inculcating a desire to learn is therefore the first thing the teacher or coach must do. Secondly, the learner must have something to focus attention on and also understand what are the important things to think about. It is a very common and frustrating problem for learners to decide what to do and what to concentrate on and a responsibility rests with the coach to direct the learner to those cues which are most appropriate at any given time. Next, the learner must establish and formulate what Gentile calls a motor plan. A motor plan is an internal idea or picture which the learner formulates describing the movements about to be executed. In a sense the motor plan is a kind of anticipation about what to do and what the consequences will be of carrying out a movement. Motor plans for beginners are likely to be very crude and not always accurate. The next stage is the physical step of actual practice in which the learner effects the motor plan. Stage five describes the process where the learner gathers information about the movements executed and the degree to which the goals were achieved. Such information will be self-generated and will also come from the coach or teacher in the form of augmented feedback. The next stage is one where the learner establishes a new motor plan, in light of feedback, in preparation for the next practice. The new plan may be totally different or else could be just a minor variation to the initial one. The seventh and final stage according to Gentile is practice once again. Stages five to seven are repeated until the learner has acquired the desired level of skill.

A model of teaching

The right-hand list in Table 1 above is quite logical and can apply to any learning situation whatever the sport or activity. Pease develops a series of guidelines for practice based on each of Gentile's learning stages. He says that first, the coach or teacher must instil into the learner a desire to learn. This may or may not be necessary depending on how interested or motivated the learner is to begin with, but Pease provides a number of ideas which could be used, e.g., show videos or films of experts in action, take the learners to a display or competition, provide models through demonstrations, allow brief participation (with little emphasis on scoring or competition), etc.. Throughout, Pease says the emphasis should be on enjoyment, the attainability of skills and the understanding of some of the difficulties to be encountered. This first stage is all about getting the learner 'hooked' and interested, establishing rough motor plans and directing the learner's attention to some of the more fundamental aspects to be addressed later.

The second stage is one where the coach helps the learner identify cues and events essential to attaining the goal. A number of approaches can be used such as manual and verbal guidance, demonstrations and hinting. Skills may be broken down into smaller parts or slowed down as appropriate. Pease makes the point that teaching cues must not be too specific and must be relevant to the stage of learning. He urges that detailed cues should be combined into larger units, e.g., in relation to the 'ready' position in tennis, the learner should be made to realise that separate points such as feet position, weight distribution, knee flexion, racket position, eye focus can all be reduced to one single event or cue: 'ready'.

In the third stage, the coach assists the learner's formation of a motor plan. Pease suggests this stage is often ignored — possibly because the coach does not have direct access to the learner's thought processes which therefore makes it a difficult process to hurdle. Techniques for helping learners here include discussing with them what they are about to try (ask them to describe their plans), forcing concentration on the feel of movements, mental practice and ensuring that demonstrations which help to create a visual picture, are clear and exact.

The next step is to provide the learner with an opportunity to practise. This involves structuring situations so that the learner can enact the internal model and concentrate on those cues which are especially relevant. A focus should be placed on safety, participation, the highlighting of relevant cues (using perhaps some of the visual techniques described in Chapter 3) and attention to the learner's performance rather than its outcome. Here, Pease draws attention to the examination of 'what went wrong' rather than emotional considerations of whether the performance was good or bad.

The fifth step mirrors Gentile's stage on attention to results. Feedback is the essence here. Pease underlines that learners should be encouraged to evaluate their own performances and internal feelings and attempt to relate the motor plan to performance. If there are differences, it is important for the learner to try and identify what went wrong rather than be told by the coach. Feedback should be informative and immediate and take into account both internal feelings (kinesthetic feedback) as well as information about movement outcome (what it looked like; how successful it was).

Stage six is linked to the last one and presents the teacher or coach with the question 'what should the learner do next'? Discussion with learners should encourage them to revise the motor plan in the hope of better performance next time. The coach might, for example, question learners about how their plan has changed, whether they understand the errors, etc.. The last stage involves practice once more, and perhaps a rethink by the coach about the tasks set or equipment used or the manner in which the learner tackles the skill again.

What does Pease's model have to offer? It highlights a number of important ideas, but as far as the present chapter is concerned two or three topics stand out. It seems important the coach should plan practice sessions within a larger framework of goals and intentions. Work should be structured in the sense that the coach should be conscious of the learner's present skills and strengths and be able to set goals which are attainable by learners. If coaches know where they have started from and they also know where they are going to, then they stand a good chance of planning in a logical and thorough manner the steps involved to get there!

Throughout Pease's model there is the implication that learners should play an active role in their own learning. Pease's view is that learning should be experiential rather than didactic. Discussion between coach and learner about what to attempt, how things felt, why did things go wrong, etc., should take place constantly. Whilst this approach may not be the 'style' adopted by some coaches it certainly concurs with recent educational thinking on learner involvement and responsibility. It makes sense that if the learner is doing the learning, then he/she should also be an active participant. Of course, this is not always possible or desirable and with beginners especially, it may be more appropriate and efficient in terms of time and energy outlay for the coach to be prescriptive and not fully involve learners in a self-analysis procedure. This view is highlighted in a subsequent chapter. One topic which Pease does not address in detail is the question of practice itself. What should be practised? How should skills be broken down? The next section looks at these matters.

Skill analysis

Before the learner is presented with a task or asked to execute a particular movement, some thought on the part of the coach must go into deciding whether the task is safe, whether it is physically demanding and interesting, whether it emphasises the relevant points and reflects the game or sport in question. Practice must be pertinent! In many cases such questions are easily and automatically answered because there are accepted and traditional methods of doing some things. Informed opinion shows the way. For example, if a novice swimmer has roughly mastered the breast stroke and can make headway without artificial support, but displays an asymmetrical leg kick, then it would make sense to isolate this component so the swimmer can concentrate on it alone. He/she might be given a hand-held float and asked to repeat a push/glide with two good leg kicks. On the other hand, it may be that the coach is fresh to the activity or a new technique has been developed (as happens for example, in artistic gymnastics or ice skating) or that traditional methods have little effect. How does the coach solve these kinds of problems? How does the coach for example, decide on the nature of practice and construct the optimal sequence of progressions for a particular skill? The research literature only provides guidelines and in any case, there is probably no one best order of practices for learning any particular activity. A useful start can be made by carrying out what is called a task analysis.

Task analysis is the systematic examination of a skill or game to decide the constituent parts, how they are organised, which cues are relevant, what the objectives are, and so on. It is a procedure which is often carried out unconsciously and as said earlier, tradition plays a large part. Many coaching texts provide comprehensive breakdowns of a skill's requirements (e.g., swimming practices commonly revolve around arm and leg actions together with breathing and co-ordination) although the 'cookbook' approach is not always the best.

There are several approaches to task analysis. One method focuses on the nature of the activity under consideration. For example, is the skill open/closed, ballistic/continuous or paced/unpaced? Analysing the skill like this allows one to make general decisions about what is or is not important. For example, if the skill is a closed one (and hence by definition is not controlled by external information) then it would make sense to concentrate on the movement requirements for practice and expect little else to be important. Thus in gymnastics this would lead to an emphasis on movement technique *per se*. If the skill was paced and therefore controlled in part by the actions of others (as in badminton or basketball) then practice would need to take account of the element of uncertainty or unpredictability.

Another approach is to use what has been called an information-processing model (see Chapter 1). This is illustrated again in Figure 14.

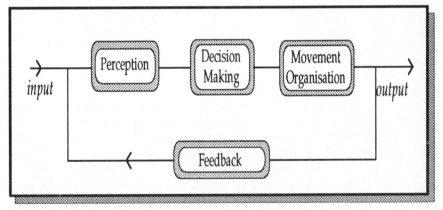

Figure 14:   A basic information-processing model.

Here, the skill is examined in relation to each of four major components. Thus, in terms of the skill's perceptual requirements consideration would be given to the number of stimuli which must be attended to (team members and opposition), the number of stimuli present (number of players, crowd, court markings) the speed of events in the display (variation in flight paths, types of ball deliveries), the extent to which they conflict (background lighting and other distractions) and so on. With regard to decision making, an appraisal is made of the number of decisions required and the speed of decision making. (In sprinting, the only decision is when to move, whereas in basketball there may be a number — dribble or pass? If dribble, which direction? If pass, to whom?, and so on.) In terms of movement organisation, an analysis would be made of the precision required, the number of limbs involved, large or small muscle groups, extent of limb co-ordination, cyclical or varying patterns of action, and so. And finally, with regard to feedback, the coach would examine the amount of feedback present (visual, auditory and movement cues may be available: do they confuse? Which is more important?); the accuracy of feedback (is it satisfactory to say simply "good" or should a detailed explanation be given?); and also the intensity (is there a pain element involved or are there other people present who may comment/distract?). Answers to these broad questions, together with knowledge of the learner's previous experience and present level of ability, will give some clue as to what is important in practice and which parts should be introduced.

One particular merit of this model is that it provides the coach with a balanced view of skill. Too often, skill is viewed primarily as a problem of movement execution alone and scant regard is paid to other, equally important elements. If the model is adhered to then all potentially important components are given consideration and nothing will be omitted from the analysis. In addition, the model provides a useful basis for error analysis. If a performer fails, then it is useful to examine each component in turn for possible causes. This approach avoids thinking once again that problems of learning are always movement ones. This point will be picked up again later when skill evaluation is discussed.

Whole and part learning

A particular problem of designing practice centres around whether relatively complex skills should be taught in their entirety or broken down into lesser, but constituent parts. Traditionally, teachers and coaches have used whole methods and part methods and also various combinations to good effect. Whole methods expose the learner to all elements of an activity (e.g., a non-swimmer might be given the freedom to try the breast stroke without any modification excepts perhaps with a buoyancy aid). Some whole methods employ modified versions which still contain the essential ingredients (e.g., mini rugby, short tennis). In contrast, part methods typically look at individual parts or elements of a skill before linking them together. Combination methods centre around a whole-part-whole approach or a progressive-part approach where elements are taught individually and gradually built up into the complete skill.

There are advantages and weaknesses with whole and part methods of practice. Splitting skills/games into smaller units serves a variety of purposes. It avoids the burden of practising elements of the whole which are perhaps too simple, time-wasting or fatiguing (e.g., the run-up in bowling when practice is really focused on ball release). It reduces the information load imposed on the learner and allows for more immediate and precise feedback. And, because part practices are simpler and less dangerous, they serve a useful role in eliminating fear which might otherwise block attempts at the whole skill. They must, of course, not be so simple that the learner becomes bored or frustrated. Learners must feel challenged and be challenged.

Research which has examined the nature of skill provides some pointers about whether skills should be broken down or left alone. With serial activities or sports such as team games where elements are 'sequentially organised' — meaning that the elements do not overlap in time (e.g., a chest pass in soccer precedes a dribble which in turn precedes a pass) — then part practice of the more difficult elements should be expected to transfer positively to the game proper. With discrete activities which involve speedy movements taking less than a second to execute (e.g., a golf swing or corner kick), then the whole method is most appropriate. Working this way ensures that the rhythm and fluidity of movement is not broken. With continuous tasks which may not have such well-defined end points as discrete ones, and where parts overlap in time and co-ordinate with one another (e.g., in the breast stroke, the arms and legs are synchronised in time), then the research evidence points in favour of the whole approach.

Scully (1988) has recently examined the problems of part practice and suggests that to be effective the cues which are highlighted in a part practice must not be isolated from the whole action. She says (p.19):

> ...in teaching the jump shot in basketball, the learner's atten-
> tion may be directed to the arms but only in as much as they
> relate to what the rest of the body is doing at the same time.
> Similarly, if cueing the learner to produce more force or speed
> in a throwing, bowling or kicking action, attention needs to
> be directed to subtle changes in trunk and other limb motion,
> in addition to changes in absolute motion components of
> the limb segments directly involved. All actions are space-time
> events and to concentrate on one aspect of this relationship
> to the exclusion of the other would destroy the fundamental
> unity of action.

The literature is quite clear on this last point. With skills in which per-formance is concerned not only with the individual components but also their integration and synchrony, then the whole approach is superior. This seems obvious because in such activities as say swimming, success depends on learning the element of co-ordination — when to kick with the legs in relation to the pull of the arms — an element which part practice may not emphasise so well. The literature does however, point to an exception to this rule and that is when the components are too complex or dangerous to allow the beginner to practise the task as a whole. In these cases, the best plan is to program practice so as to develop some proficiency in the separate components choosing components that are as nearly independent of each other as possible and then alternating between part and whole practice.

A number of other factors are also important in the choice between whole and part-type practice. Assuming the beginner has the right set to learn and is motivated to 'play the game' or 'have a go' straight away, then even though the learner will not be fully skilled, an attempt should be made to present the whole skill as near as is practicable, simply to encourage interest and maintain enthusiasm. Such an approach helps establish motor plans for action and also helps define the objectives of the skill in question. Mini-sport is one way to get beginners playing the game they want to play, whilst keeping rules, skills, fitness demands, etc., within acceptable boundaries. Once beginners have been introduced in this manner, they are in a position to accept more readily the need for specific part practices and drills. And it should be emphasised again that when parts are extracted from the whole for separate practice, they should be seen by the learner to be relevant and meaningful. If this is not obvious then the coach should make a conscious effort to justify part practice by perhaps talking about when the parts are required in the game or how the part is a necessary sub-component of a more difficult element. This point is very important. Learners must be kept informed and understand the 'why' of practice. If they do, then they will accept more readily the need for practice, appreciate its contribution in the whole scheme of things, and the coach can consequently expect far greater transfer from part to whole.

Two other points are also worthy of mention. People are individuals and different individuals learn in different ways. The point was made in a previous chapter that some people may prefer a lengthy account from their coach about the skill, whilst others may prefer to see demonstrations. Similarly, some learners prefer a progressive, part approach whilst others favour an attempt at the whole skill immediately. The literature talks about 'sequential' and 'holistic' learners. The coach should use this knowledge — it could prove a powerful force with some people. Finally, the coach's teaching style may suit one approach particularly; it would be unwise to discard proven methods without careful consideration of alternative ones.

Even learning theories differ on the value of part and whole learning (see Chapter 1). Basically, there are no hard and fast rules, but a number of general guidelines:

1.   A whole approach is better for maintaining skill coherence and learner enthusiasm. The general idea — the whole — should be grasped by the learner before complex details are introduced.

2. Part practice is desirable when the whole skill is too complicated, dangerous, or tiring to attempt in its complete form.
3. Parts should be manageable and understandable to the learner. They should present challenge and relate meaningfully to the whole skill.
4. Part practices must be followed by co-ordination into the whole.
5. In a group situation where many learners are involved, part practice may increase the degree of participation.

Sequencing of practice

It can be argued that the process of breaking skills into smaller parts must take place within the context of the whole skill. In most sports the elements are dependent upon one another (e.g., in soccer, ball reception might lead to a dribble which in turn leads to passing). In practice therefore, the sequencing of the elements should not be a random affair. Part practices should form part of a hierarchy in which those taught first 'feed' into more complicated ones which in turn lead the learner to even more detailed ones. There should be a logical progression from basic, simple skills which are prerequisites for more complicated tasks, through to the final skill or game. This is not to propose a rigid, inflexible approach — deviations, modifications, repetitions, regressions which are needed to solve individual problems will occur — but the coach or teacher must devise a framework in which effective instruction can take place. The following example demonstrates how a new footwork movement pattern would be introduced to an expert badminton player, and shows clearly a logical sequence.

1. Use a video of a top player and/or give a shadow demonstration of the new movements.
2. Allow the players to shadow the movement.
3. Introduce the shuttle so the player is forced to move across court, play a stroke and recover to base.
4. Introduce an opponent so the player is put under pressure. Etc., etc..

Practice variability and overlearning

Two important principles of learning have not been addressed so far. The first is the notion of variability in practice. Research has shown repeatedly that in the learning of some tasks (e.g., throwing/striking a ball for accuracy as in cricket or volleyball), variable practice results in greater accuracy and consistency than specific practice. This finding is more marked with children than adults. For example, Carson & Weingard (1979) studied children throwing a bean bag to a target on the floor. Children had over a 100 trials using either the same bean bag every trial or else using a bag selected on each trial from one of four bags of different weights. After practice it was found that the group given variability of training with bags of different weights were significantly more accurate using a bean bag of a novel weight than were the children only exposed to a bag of a single weight. In the learning of a catching task, say slip-fielding in cricket, this would suggest that people should be exposed to deliveries from different angles, at different speeds and varying flight paths and not simply a constant throw to their hands. Why this should be so is explained very well by schema theory mentioned before. Quite simply, if a large part of skill learning is concerned with the acquisition of 'rules' i.e., the ways and means of carrying out a skill—process involved — then the richer and more diverse the practice the more effective it should be. This view fits in well with what we know about open skills, for here the task is always changing and thus the learner needs to be adaptable to new and unexpected things. The interesting thing about schema theory is that it also predicts variable practice should be better with closed skills. The idea of practice variability ties in nicely with modern thinking on the importance of individual learning, but it does have its critics. Whiting (1982: p.12) argues that early learning should be marked by stability so that the learner understands better what is required:

> ... the introduction of variations in environmental conditions should be postponed in the process of learning until an adequate 'image of the act' has been developed under one of the many conditions under which the act has eventually to be executed, i.e., 'the image of the act' has first to be developed as a holistic unit, a gestalt, before it can be manipulated to serve acts under changed conditions.

It seems that a compromise may be best through adopting Whiting's view about beginners, but as soon as the learner has a broad idea about skill, he/she should be made to practise in a way which mirrors the sport proper. So, in team games for example, the learner should quickly be introduced to key elements such as competition, teamwork, decision making, tactical play, etc..

The topic of overlearning also deserves mention. It is suggested by many researchers that performers never actually achieve their true physiological and psychological potentials. Their true maximum remains an elusive goal — one of which they may be unaware. The only way to approach close to this goal is to train long, hard and in the most appropriate manner. For many people though, the time and effort required is either practically impossible or else limited through boredom, injury or fatigue. The fact is that if people can practise beyond the point when they have apparently reached their maximum level of success — and this could mean working on an action (e.g., a tennis serve) many thousands of times — then they are rewarded by slight improvements in performance. In addition, overlearning — as it is called — ensures performance becomes more consistent, less resistant to failure under stress and better remembered over time. It is considered for example, that recent success by Chinese gymnasts is due largely to overlearning techniques. It is also likely that the technical consistency demonstrated by many world class track and field athletes is partly due to the incredible number of times they have practised. If practical, it makes sense for coaches to 'take on board' the principle of overlearning even though there will be attendant problems of time, money and facilities. It goes without saying of course, that only movements which are technically correct should be overlearned!

Active or passive learning?

Mental practice

One of the curious things about learning is that it can apparently take place without recourse to physical practice. People sometimes improve from one training session to the next even though they have not practised in between times. One reason could be they have 'mentally practised' during the interval — covertly gone through the activity in their mind — and this has supplemented physical practice. Many international-level athletes testify to the value of mentally going through an action in their 'mind's eye' before an important event or competition. The research literature on mental practice is very extensive and demonstrates quite clearly that under certain conditions it can have a beneficial effect — not so much as actual practice, but certainly more than no practice at all (for example, Hird, *et al.*, 1991).

In one particular study, three groups of people were chosen to learn a 'pursuit rotor' task (this requires the person to visually track a target moving in a circular manner with a hand held stylus). One group physically practised over a period of time, one group did not practise at all and the third group were instructed to simply visualise the task in their head. At the end of the training period the mental practice group had learned to perform almost as successfully as the physical practice group! Why should this be the case? The answer is not entirely clear. It is possible that mental practice allows the learner an opportunity to work on the cognitive or intellectual parts of a skill (e.g., trying to understand the best way of beating a zone defence system in basketball) — components which might not normally receive the same kind of attention as with physical practice. This view has received some experimental support and is also supported by the finding that mental practice sometimes works well with novices when cognitive problems are to the fore. Another explanation is that mental practice causes a physiological training effect in the sense that it invokes the same physiological processes underlying movement selection, movement execution and feedback. This idea too has received a little scientific support. A more feasible explanation is that mental practice causes a number of other changes to take place such as reducing the performer's anxiety level, preparing him/her psychologically for action and clarifying immediate goals. It may be that secondary changes such as these allow the individual to perform better. This idea certainly agrees with the views of many athletes, but the exact cause/s is still unknown.

Mental practice is part of a growing subject which centres on psychological training and preparation. It cannot be dealt with seriously in just a couple of paragraphs and will be considered in more depth in a later chapter. For the present, three issues should be raised.

1.   Mental practice hinges on the effectiveness of skill transfer (see later in this chapter) and it follows therefore that all the criteria underpinning positive transfer — specificity, reality, etc. — must also be satisfied if mental practice is to be of any value.

2.   Mental practice is a complex process. Many expressions are used such as visualisation, imagery, covert rehearsal and they all have different meanings and applications. Different senses can be used for mental practice; each for different purposes and in different ways. In addition, one has to learn how to mentally practice. It is a skill itself which requires practice and experience and takes time. To use it therefore requires a commitment and interest on the part of the coach/teacher as well as the learner.

3.   Thirdly, the effectiveness of any kind of mental practice seems to depend on the sport, situation and the individual. Mental rehearsal may work very well for some players before competition whilst others may find it of value only as a training exercise (perhaps during a lay-off through injury). Some people may find that a combination of different forms of mental practice is most effective whilst others may struggle to concentrate on any technique.

We shall return to this topic in Chapter 7.

Direct or guided learning?

Mental practice is, by default, a passive kind of practice. In one sense, physical practice can also be passive, i.e., when the learner is told directly what to do and is given little encouragement to try things out or assess his/her own performance. Whilst such as approach has a place, especially when the degree of danger attached is high, support for an active or guided approach to learning is very strong. It might be useful for a moment to look at a classic study which examined the perceptual-motor development of young kittens for it highlights the value of active learning. In this study, two kittens were held in a circular carousel arrangement in which one could walk unaided whilst the other was carried around in a basket moved by the first kitten. Because of the mechanical linkage between the two kittens, both received exactly the same kind of visual stimulation during their time in the carousel. Of course the active one also received internal, kinesthetic feedback whereas the passive one did not.

At the end of the testing period, the active kittens had developed normal motor co-ordination and could successfully execute simple tasks, whereas the passive ones failed. The point in describing this study — which has also been repeated in modified form with both animals and humans — is to underline the critical importance of allowing the individuals to play an active role in the learning process.

Other lines of reasoning support the same view. The information-processing view of human performance sees the individual not as a passive receiver of information who acts in a stereotyped and predictable manner, but as an active searcher for information who anticipates events and actions and tries to make the best sense of the data available. Young children behave in much the same way as they explore the world about them. The child psychologist Piaget (e.g., Piaget & Inhelder, 1967), was of the opinion that a child's intellectual development stems directly from active contact with the immediate environment. And recent educational thinking on guided-discovery or problem-solving approaches to learning also support this view with some studies providing clear, supporting evidence (see Drowatzky, 1981).

The process of involving the learner in the learning process includes a number of strategies: use of trial and error practice, helping the learner with the opportunity to analyse performance, discussing how to tackle problems with the coach/teacher, and so on. To an extent this is really a matter of coaching or teaching style. For some coaches, notably those who adhere to the 'Inner Game' philosophy (see Chapter 7) it is important for the learner to take responsibility and play an active part in learning. For many coaches, however, it may be inappropriate. For advanced learners working on highly specific movements or for potentially danger-ous skills, a direct form of coaching may be more appropriate.

Use of simulators

The learner's involvement is partly reduced when manual guidance is adopted to help overcome complex or dangerous movements. With the use of simulators, the whole action can be removed. Simulators attempt to mimic a procedure or movement in some artificial way. Aircraft simulators which mirror the flying conditions experienced in even the largest of jet aircraft are commonly used in pilot training schedules. Such devices are designed to reduce costs, save time and where appropriate, provide training in safe conditions. Although mainly found in the industrial/commercial fields, they do feature in sport also. Machines have been devised to constrain the club in a golf swing, to project cricket and tennis balls with varying flight characteristics, to teach rowing on dry land and even dummies have been used to provide targets for blocking practice in American football. In addition, windsurfing simulators are very popular, cross-country ski exercisers can be purchased which 'groove' technique and computer games can now be purchased which simulate almost every sport in existence! A recently designed 'ski fit machine' is said to "... accurately simulate the motion of downhill skiing, and help to increase aerobic fitness, while improving co-ordination and exercise of the appropriate muscle joints" (*Sports Industry*, 1991: p.16). Claims such as these are rarely tested and it would appear there is much scope for research into the actual value of simulators. In terms of skill learning, it is likely that simulators are of value only to the extent that they mirror real conditions and allow transfer to the game or movement proper. Apart from one or two obvious cases (e.g., dry ski matting) the evidence would suggest their value is very limited. It is worth saying too that they must also be cost effective and in many cases it may prove too costly for a club to purchase, say, a high-tech bowling machine or an expensive computer.

Transfer of learning

Practically all learning is based on some form of transfer — the application of previous experience to present learning. It is thought we rarely learn a totally new skill after the early years of childhood — new skills invariably arise out of previous experiences. A central assumption in most practice situations is that whatever is learned during practice will have a beneficial effect at a subsequent time.

Positive transfer, as it is called, is assumed to take place in many areas of sporting endeavour. For example, a course of physical conditioning in the weights room is assumed to make the player fitter for the game situation. Feelings and emotions heightened during the pre-match team talk are meant to be carried onto the field of play. And techniques practised during training are meant to carry over to the complete skill and polish the individual's overall level of performance. In judo for example, resistance on the part of the defender is critical. If experienced and overcome in practice, then it is easier to overcome in competition.

In contrast, *negative transfer* is an unwanted agent and refers to the inhibiting effect that a practice or previous activity has on current learning. An American footballer who takes up rugby may be penalised for 'blocking', which is an integral part of football but is illegal in rugby. Here, a previously learned action intrudes to the detriment of performance in a new sport. A similar type of 'interference' happens in racket sports when players proficient in one sport, say tennis, attempt to learn another, say badminton. Initially, they may swing the racket incorrectly and fail to take account of the different flight characteristics of the shuttle. Their performance suffers as a consequence. In situations like this the initial negative influences are often overtaken by positive transfer.

Decisions about how practice is designed must be based on the assumption of positive transfer. For example, in passing drills the coach expects something to carry over to performance in the game of basketball. In springboard diving, the practice of particular moves on the trampoline is expected to benefit the diver when actually in the pool situation. It is clear that techniques like this work otherwise they would have been discarded long ago. The interesting question is whether they always work and whether they are the best techniques? It would be useful to know under what conditions transfer is maximised so that best use can be made of practice time. Such knowledge might also minimise the problems of negative transfer, where previous learning has a detrimental effect on current learning. Research in the area is quite considerable and has examined many different kinds of tasks ranging from laboratory-type skills to more realistic sporting skills. The research has yielded different and sometimes contradictory findings, but three points do emerge:

1. Positive transfer between two skills is small and positive, unless they are practically identical.
2. The amount of transfer depends largely on the similarity between the two skills.
3. Positive transfer between two skills depends on the degree to which the first skill has been learned.

Let us examine each in turn. Firstly, point one. The literature shows that motor skills transfer very little between one another, even when they are apparently very similar. In one study for example, people learned how to execute a volleyball pass before they learned a basketball tip for accuracy. They also practised a badminton volley before learning a tennis volley. In both cases, learning the first action had little positive value in learning the second. The same is also found when one particular action is used but it is practised slowly first and then at normal speed. The reason for such findings is thought to be based on what is referred to as the 'specificity of skill' hypothesis. This proposes that skills are defined by a profile of 'abilities' and that a person's ability to learn and perform a skill depends upon whether the person possesses the right mix of abilities appropriate to that skill. Skills which are just slightly different (e.g., crawl leg action in the water and on the pool side) may have little effect on each other because the learner may have the abilities necessary for one but not the other. The reader may wish to apply the same principle to the area of fitness. Here, it is known that different sports require different fitness profiles and so a player fit for one sport (say football) may not be fit for another (say hockey).

Let us now take the second point: namely, that transfer depends largely on the degree of similarity between the two situations or skills in question. The greater the number of elements identical between the two the greater the transfer. This idea is intuitively appealing and is supported by the S-R or association theory of learning discussed in Chapter 1. The word 'element' is important here. What does it mean? Are elements something to do with the physical actions involved (e.g., arm action in a swimming stroke) or the stimulus cues in the display (e.g., the manner in which a ball or shuttle travels) or perhaps principles of play (e.g., movement off the ball, zone defence)? The literature has not really solved this one. What seems important is that when the coach analyses a skill for the purpose of breaking it down into part practices, he/she should assess all possible aspects for relevance and not just the physical movements involved. So, elements such as competition, co-operation or combat which are central to the whole skill should also appear in practice. Skills should be taught so they are transferable from one situation to another. All those variables which appear in the complete skill — movement, speed, form, body control, agility, decision-making, effort, concentration, relaxation, etc., should be introduced in practice. In addition, it is critical for the coach to underline not only similarities between practice and competition, but also the differences which exist. The learner should be guided into assessing where the similarities begin and end. In this way the learner should become a much more discriminating and hence skilled performer.

The third point is really a matter of common sense. One would hardly expect transfer to take place if there is nothing to transfer! It follows that learners are better able to benefit from past experience if that experience is substantial. In terms of part practices for example, in order to maximise their transfer value the learner must have repeated the part a sufficient number of times to have fully understood and acquired a 'feel' for it. Thus, swimming just a few lengths of breast stroke legs would be insufficient. The learner should expect to practise hundreds of lengths for there to be a transfer effect.

To summarise, the weight of evidence points to the limited and uncertain nature of transfer between two tasks. Coaches and teachers should be especially guarded in expecting transfer to take place automatically. A question mark should always be placed against skills practices which occur out of the game context or outwith the physical environment of the game proper. Similarly there is a need to be cautious about the manner in which skills are broken down for part practice. In addition, if transfer depends on the similarity between part and whole practice then the coach should analyse the requirements of the whole skill to enable him/her to break it down into units which are as close as possible to the whole skill.

Shaping behaviour

Some sports techniques are simple to acquire and can be performed with a degree of success after relatively few number of attempts (e.g., javelin hand grip, underarm volleyball serve). It is unlikely these would be broken down into lesser parts. Others however, cannot be learned easily because they are too complicated or dangerous. Take, for example, a diving routine or a difficult gymnastic stunt. These have to be reduced and simplified in some way.

One way of doing this is to break the action into simple steps so the learner can work progressively through each one. Each distinct part of the action is then thought of as a link in a chain. The performer first learns one link, then adds a second link and practises the two together. Then a third link can be added and all three practised in sequence, and so on until the chain is complete. This is the classic notion of progressive-part practice, sometimes called chaining. In chaining, each part is practised just as it will be performed in the finished technique. This method can only be used effectively with serial-type activities.

Another method is called shaping (described in the Introduction). Shaping is the method whereby a complex movement is taught through the gradual shaping or changing of simpler movements. It is especially appropriate for complicated techniques found in closed sports such as trampolining and gymnastics which are sometimes impossible to break down in a logical manner. Shaping is not unlike trial and error learning where movements are eliminated and others steadily altered until the desired one is established. It is worth illustrating this with a couple of examples. Most skiers aspire to perfect parallel turns but, for most people, this is too complex to tackle straight away. One way of approaching this is to teach firstly a simple snow plough glide. Once mastered, a turn can be incorporated first in one direction then the other. Following this, the element of 'unweighting' can be introduced which allows the learner to bring the skis together for the turn. With practice the skis can be bought parallel earlier in the turn until both traverse and turn are accomplished with the legs roughly parallel. In this example, the whole skill has gradually been formed by successively developing simpler ones. In women's gymnastics, perfecting new routines on the asymmetric bars presents particular problems of safety, and so on. Take, for example, the 'straddle back to catch' illustrated in Figure 15.

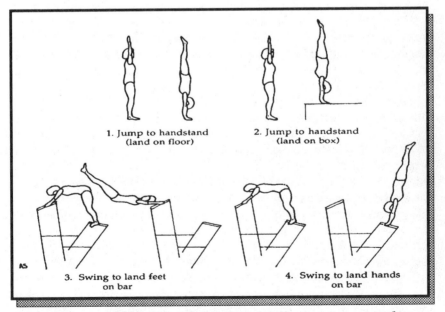

Figure 15:   **A sequence of practices leading up to a complex gymnastic movement.**

In the first stage the gymnast jumps into a handstand to land with hands where the feet were placed, with support from the coach. Secondly, the gymnast attempts the same movement but without support. Next, the gymnast jumps to handstand but moves slightly backward to land higher on a box section. Fourthly, the gymnast tries this without support from the coach. Next, the gymnast transfers to the bars to adopt a position with hands holding the upper bar and feet resting on the lower one. She then swings forward and returns to rest with feet on the lower bar. The next stage is the same swing again but, with the coach standing by, the gymnast releases the high bar to catch the lower one on the return swing. Finally, this is tried without coach support. In this example, the coach has devised a number of simpler actions where each develops naturally from the preceding one, thus presenting the learner with small steps in difficulty every time. With careful thought and ingenuity, this method can be applied to most situations and techniques which are too complicated to learn as a whole.

Both of these examples demonstrate skills being shaped through the successive practice of easier but changing actions. For the technique to work, each stage must be attainable and also rewarded. Normally, the learner's intrinsic feedback would provide knowledge of success, but with younger or less experienced people the coach would add his/her own words of encouragement.

Specificity of skill

Before leaving the topic of transfer a few words should be said on what has been referred to as the 'generality — specificity' issue. The research literature is awash with studies designed to answer whether we transfer just specific things from the past to the present or whether we can generalise ideas, principles and skills and apply our experience to much wider settings. The 'general' hypothesis would predict for example, that someone who excels in one fast ball game should also achieve in others. The 'specificity' argument would disagree with this and say the skills required across sports are so different as to negate any positive transfer. There is not a clear answer to this question. Evidence supports both views. However, it is widely accepted that as the learner becomes more skilful, techniques and strategies required for success become more distinctive and hence practice must be more specific. At the novice level, it is possible to shift basic skills such as hitting or throwing a ball from one sport to another with a degree of success. Some principles of play common to a number of sports (e.g., wall pass, faking, moving into space) are potentially transferable. Similarly, some attitudes and feelings can be transposed from activity to activity.

The best conclusion to be drawn from the literature is that skill is, by and large, specific. However, the coach should try to harness the learner's past experience by making realistic links where they exist. The transfer of general actions or principles may be possible in early learning, but as skill develops transfer is overtaken by the acquisition of specific techniques, strategies, and so on.

Error is the price of skill

Few people enjoy failure and most strive to make a success of all they do. The science of ergonomics specifically aims to reduce the chances of making errors in our everyday lives through the good design of equipment/everyday objects. In terms of skill, guidance is intended to point the learner's way towards correct performance and how to do things efficiently and accurately. Learners are not normally forced into error situations intentionally or allowed to repeat mistakes.

The learner will, of course, make mistakes on the way to excellence and the coach will recognise them but, by and large, the practising of mistakes and incorrect actions is rarely encouraged in the coaching/learning process. An interesting question is, should the coach concentrate on the negative side of skilled action and is this a profitable approach to skill learning? Do people learn from making errors? Should they be guided into making errors? Many authors have addressed this issue and at least one theory of learning supports the 'practice of errors' idea.

It could be argued that guidance is too one-sided and the process of instructing correct movements alone gives the learner no clues about alternative solutions. We could say that knowledge of correct actions is incomplete if the learner is not given the opportunity to define them against alternatives.

Errors are a natural result of trial and error learning and many teachers and coaches argue that people learn from their errors. This seems especially relevant in outdoor activities such as orienteering and sailing. For example, in sailing the learner picks up a lot of useful information about a boat's capabilities, wind patterns and emergency drill through capsizing the dinghy — even when unplanned. Similarly, in orienteering a novice will learn salient principles of navigation by making fundamental mistakes in say, pace judgement or use of the compass. To take another example, the novice rock climber's confidence is increased immeasurably if he/she relaxes hold on the rock and takes his/her weight on the rope above. In this way it is learned that the rope really will hold if he/she falls! There are bound to be similar instances in other sports, but the important question is whether the coach should actively encourage such errors to take place. For example, when coaching a volleyball serve, should the learner be made to serve both short into the net and long outside the court, even though the game demands neither of these options? To take an example in trampolining, would it be a useful lead-up to straight bouncing to give the novice experience of bouncing all over the bed rather than just in the centre? It may seem a little strange to answer this question in the affirmative, but a current theory of motor learning called schema theory (Schmidt, 1982) supports the idea of 'error' practice.

Schema theory concentrates on how people change when they learn. The view is that people learn 'rules' which govern the manner in which movements are organised and executed. People do not learn movements *per se*. Rather, they learn the principles (unconsciously) about how to move. Rules are acquired through active participation, feedback and experience. Furthermore, the more varied the practice, the more strongly the rules are established. In this context, errors are an integral part of the learning process, adding to its variety and so strengthening the basis for skilled movement.

This notion is supported by some experimental findings and there is also anecdotal evidence from coaches. In a much quoted example, an American baseball coach forces the pitchers to aim the ball wide of the plate during practice in the belief that their perception of correct aiming will become more acute. Research in education supports this kind of idea. It is thought, for example, to be a good teaching strategy to present learners with alternative ways to solve problems together with an opportunity to practise them. They must however, also be given knowledge of the correct solutions (Holding, 1965). Holding argues that "...knowledge of the correct response is incomplete if there is no opportunity to define it against the alternatives..." (p.51). He describes clearly what is meant by an error and makes an important distinction between errors and alternative movements. He suggests that guiding learners into alternative ways of solving problems does not imply they have made a mistake, rather, they have just practised an alternative response pattern. Whether this idea holds for all sports is questionable. One must always guard against the possibility of developing bad habits through continued error practice, but it does present an interesting, novel and possibly very effective coaching technique. This matter is discussed further by Sharp (1988, 1989).

Duration and frequency of practice

One of the classic areas of motor learning research concerns the spacing or distribution of practice. How long should a practice session be? How frequently should practice sessions occur? Should practice sessions be grouped together (e.g., beginner swimming lessons every day of the week) or spaced apart (lessons once a week)? Unlike the research on physical conditioning which gives clear guidelines on strategies for improving, say, cardio-respiratory fitness, no such generalisations are possible for skill acquisition. Furthermore, much of the research has attempted to explain skill learning in terms of laboratory-type tasks, and much is contradictory.

It would seem that the kinds of practical considerations listed below should play the biggest role in connection with the spacing and timing of practice.

1.   A minimum time is essential for warm up, to establish an appropriate working relationship and level of motivation, and to ensure that some learning has occurred.

2. Practice is often limited by finance, time and facilities. A coach, for example, may only be free to work with the athletes for a single two-hour session each week. Or a teacher may be constrained by the school timetable to work with children, say, only 3 times a week for 45 minutes each session.
3. The amount of time spent working with youngsters or beginners should be limited because their attention span is generally limited.
4. Some activities are too demanding physically to allow lengthy practice and a minimal recovery period is essential if accidents are not to occur or bad technique be grooved.
5. There will always be a maximum period dictated by physical and/or psychological fatigue, both of which will depend on the skill in question and the experience of the learner.

What seems important is that the coach or teacher gives priority to the 'quality' of practice within the time permitted. This will involve structuring practices correctly (shaping, chaining, etc.) and setting realistic targets — however simple — which can be reached by learners. In addition, learners will naturally pace themselves with regard to fitness and interest and this can serve as a guide for the coach. So long as the learner maintains interest and remembers what has been learned from session to session, and is given the encouragement/opportunity to work in between times, then the question of spacing or massing practice has little relevance.

Instructional considerations

If practice is to be effective then it must take place within a well-structured and safe environment. There are a number of considerations which apply to most sports and to all learners. Firstly, practice must be safe. In certain sports — especially outdoor activities — safety is a prime feature and clear guidelines established by the governing body or teaching establishment help the instructor plan practice accordingly (e.g., novice orienteers may work in pairs on their first visit to a forest). In other sports safety factors relating to use of equipment, slipperiness of surfaces, warm up procedures, etc. also play an important part. For example, a number of groups working in the same area would be spread apart so as not to interfere with each other. Similarly, gymnastic equipment would not be placed close to walls, windows, or other items.

Practice must be planned, thought out well in advance and must be given a purpose. Purpose and direction help to motivate learners, controlling those who may not be so well motivated intrinsically, as well as ensuring maximum use is made of the time available. Generally, learners should be made aware of why they are practising certain things (e.g., "This practice will show you why it is vital to take advantage of the space between members of the opposition"). The coach's goals should be in synchrony with the needs and expectations of the learners and practice should be related to the game situation/whole skill. Otherwise, learners may well become very skilled 'jugglers of the ball' but lack the ability to use those skills in the game.

Establishing appropriate goals is based on sound preparation which takes place in advance of actual practice. Knowing what equipment is required, how court areas need to be split, what tasks will be given to learners, how groups will be divided (e.g., groups of three working together initially followed by 3 v 3 practices), etc., are matters which, if dealt with at the right time make for efficiency and go a long way to establishing good learner/coach/teacher relationships. Goals must also be planned ahead. Practice must have clear and simple intentions. Learning is a long-term affair: practice sessions which attempt too much will just waste everyone's time.

Having established a set of intentions, the coach or teacher should be prepared to adjust and modify them as appropriate. Through observation, changes may need to be made to say the composition of groups, the layout of equipment or the complexity of the task (e.g., reduce a 3 v 3 practice to a 2 v 2). Good planning should require few dramatic changes, but things do occur (e.g., a gymnast displays a particular fault which needs to be avoided) which may require a rethink or change of plan, and the coach must be prepared to modify practice accordingly.

Once practice is underway, the coach or teacher must consider his/her ongoing involvement and know how to communicate effectively with the group. As a guide, the continuity of practice should not be broken too frequently. We have already said that practice is the medium for learning and practice is what learners want to do — they do not wish to have their work interrupted constantly to listen to unnecessary comments from the coach. Before practice is stopped, the coach or teacher should know what he/she is going to say or do next. He/she should move in advance to a position where all can be seen and heard. The use of clear and obvious commands (e.g., "Stop", "Begin") directs learners easily, saves time and helps establish a working atmosphere. Simple steps such as kneeling down to ensure the same eye-level contact are quite critical. A coach working with few people or perhaps more experienced learners may adopt a 'softer' approach to communication. However, the coach must be heard above the normal sounds of practice which are often magnified by the poor acoustics in sports halls.

If the group has stopped to observe a demonstration then it too must be seen by everyone. And if the angle of observation is critical (e.g., demonstration of height gained in a gymnastic vault from a lateral view) then people must be positioned accordingly. Demonstrations should be preceded by a description and everyone directed to the essential element/s before the demonstration begins.

Throughout practice, the coach should be evaluating the work of learners and asking certain questions. Are things safe? Is the equipment appropriate? Are tasks being carried out in accordance with instructions? Do the learners understand what is required? Are they being challenged? Are they working purposefully? etc., etc.. If practice is to be meaningful the coach's role as an observer and analyst is critical. Providing praise, giving feedback, examining the work of individuals, looking for common problems, etc., are part of an ongoing process which helps to make practice effective and interesting.

Finally, it is worth raising at this stage the matter of attention demand. Practice serves no useful purpose if the learner doesn't know what to attend to or is confused because there are too many conflicting things to think about or do. If there is one thing that research on human performance is clear about, it is that people are very limited in the number of things they can handle at any one time (e.g., the number of technical points relating to say a backward somersault or the number of people involved in a team sport). People can also be confused by the complexity of the task (e.g., a beginner introduced to the game of volleyball) even when it appears easy to the coach/teacher.

The fact is that people, especially those new to an activity or sport, have a limited attention span and memory capacity for short periods of time. This has important implications for the manner in which practice is structured. For example, techniques which are thought by the coach to be too complex or difficult should be broken down into smaller parts or 'shaped' from simpler versions. Given that a technique contains a number of different criteria, the coach should identify the sequence in which they should be introduced and then set about presenting them one at a time. For example, a sprint start practice might focus simply on foot placement. The next time it might look at hand positioning. As practice continues and the learner begins to 'handle' a number of items (without prompting from the coach) the learner's attention can be bought back to aspects which may have been forgotten or need refining. An essential skill is the coach's ability to identify, from what may appear to be a multitude of errors, which is the most pertinent and focus the learner's attention on this one alone. The observant coach or teacher who has a sound technical knowledge will be able to isolate errors which may be fundamental to a number of other problems and difficulties.

Lastly, from an organisational point of view the coach should determine whether the learner's attention is being distracted because of irrelevant things such as the sun or background noise. The sun may obscure a demonstration, background noises may mask instructions, equipment may be unsafely positioned, fellow learners may be chatting and so on. The whole practice environment should be geared to ensuring that learners devote complete attention to the task at hand. Practices which are interesting, enjoyable, relevant and safe are fundamental to the skill learning process. The interested reader may wish to refer to Shedden and Armstrong (1985) for information on these topics.

Summary
1. Breaking skills down into smaller parts has a number of advantages:
    a. information load is reduced;
    b. attention to vital aspects is enhanced;
    c. physical fatigue is minimised;
    d. time is not wasted on the practice of unimportant aspects.
2. The successful breakdown of skills depends on the extent to which the parts relate to the whole.
3. Research on whole and part learning indicates the following:
    a. positive transfer between part and whole skill practice can be expected with skills which are serial in nature;
    b. discrete activities should not be broken into smaller parts;
    c. with skills in which the parts are synchronised in time, whole practice is favoured.
4. Learners benefit more from practices which resemble the whole game or skill. Improvers and experts are better able to 'bridge the gap' between part and whole practices.
5. The design of practices should acknowledge that both learners and coaches have accustomed ways of learning/coaching. Some prefer a part-type of method whilst others the whole approach.
6. Methods of guidance, e.g., visual demonstration, direct the learner towards the correct things to do.
7. It is argued that learning is incomplete if the learner is only aware of the correct techniques; the learner must have knowledge of alternatives (errors, mistakes) in order to fully define correct technique.
8. The schema theory of motor learning focuses on the learning of 'rules' as the basis for skilled performance. The acquisition of sets of rules or schema depends in part upon the variety of experiences gained by the learner. The practice of errors enhances variety and is therefore a positive stage in learning.
9. Positive transfer takes place when present learning is enhanced through previous skills. Negative transfer takes place when previous learning has a detrimental effect on current learning.
10. Positive transfer is frequently taken for granted. Transfer must be worked for rather than expected.
11. Research on the transfer of learning reveals that transfer between two skills is often low and positive. The degree of 'similarity' between the two skills is thought to be the most important factor determining the amount of transfer.
12. Coaches should be cautious in their expectations of transfer between part practices and whole skills (e.g., breast stroke leg action on land and the complete stroke in water).
13. Task analysis is the process of assessing the important elements which go to make up a skill. The elements may be diffuse in nature

and include perceptual, strategic, motor and feedback components.

14. Both coaching practice and learning theory support the notion of variability in practice as opposed to the practice of specific movements in unchanging situations.

15. The principle of variability is especially applicable to novices and young children. In addition, it holds true for both open skills in which the display is constantly changing and closed skills where the display is more static.

16. Overlearning is the process of repeated practice beyond the stage when learners have — apparently — reached their best performance.

17. Overlearning is dictated by practical considerations such as time, expense and motivation, but pays off in terms of increased performance level, consistency of performance and enhanced memory.

Discussion questions

Refer all of the questions below to a sport in which you are most familiar, either as a performer or coach/teacher.

1. In relation to the whole/part issue:
   a. Are there accepted methods in your sport where one approach is always adopted?
   b. Do the textbook methods always work?
   c. Do you give much thought to the problem of breaking skills down into smaller parts?
   d. Do you think that some of the accepted procedures used by coaches in your sport are limited, e.g., too much time is devoted to skills practices at the expense of their contribution in the game?
   e. How difficult is it to introduce beginners to your sport without modifying it considerably?
   f. Do you ever see people experience difficulties when attempting to put skills which are practised in isolation, into the game?

2. Do you think the normal level of variability which learners experience in your sport (e.g., playing partners, different equipment, varying weather) is sufficient and desirable?

3. Do you think learners would benefit from more effort on the part of coaches or teachers to increase the 'variability' factor?

4. Do you think there are any advantages of practising beyond the point when the athlete has achieved the set goals?

5. What are the disadvantages of too much practice?

6. Do you think learners could do a little better given that conditions were slightly different? What conditions would need to change?

7. In relation to the matter of errors in learning:
   a. Are they a natural part of the learning process?
   b. Are they desirable? Should they be eliminated as much as possible?

    c.   How beneficial is it for learners to examine the reasons for failure?

    d.   Schema theory emphasises the value in coaching 'slightly wrong' movements: e.g., throwing wide of the target. What do you think of this 'active' method of dealing with errors?

8.   Can you think of an example where a sport learned previously by someone is detrimental to the acquisition of skill in your sport?

9.   How sure are you that the manner in which you break down skills for practice is the best way of building up skill level?

References

Carson, L.M. & Weingard, R.L. (1979) Motor schema formation and retention in young children: A test of Schmidt's schema theory. *Journal of Motor Behavior,* **11**, 247–251.

Drowatzky, J.N. (1981) *Motor learning: Principles and practices (2nd. Ed.).* Minneapolis, Minnesota: Burgess Publishing Company.

Gentile, A.M. (1972) A working model of skill acquisition with application to teaching. *Quest,* **17**, 3–23.

Hird, J.S., Landers, D.M., Thomas, J.R., & Horan, J.J. (1991) Physical practice is superior to mental practice in enhancing cognitive and motor task performance. *Journal of Sport and Exercise Psychology.* **8**, 281–293.

Holding, D.H. (1965) *Principles of training.* London: Pergamon Press.

Pease, D.A. (1977) A teaching model for motor skill acquisition. *Motor skills: Theory into practice,* **1**, 2, 104–112.

Piaget, J. & Inhelder, B. (1967) *The child's conception of space.* New York: W.W. Norton.

Schmidt, R.A. (1988) *Motor control and learning: A behavioral emphasis.* Champaign, Illinois: Human Kinetics Publishers.

Scully, D.M. (1988) Visual perception of human movement: The use of demonstrations in teaching motor skills. *British Journal of Physical Education (Research Supplement),* **19**, 6.

Shedden, J. & Armstrong, M. (1985) *Effective coaching.* Level 2 Resource Pack. Leeds: The National Coaching Foundation.

Sharp, R.H. (1988) Error is the price of skill. *British Journal of Physical Education,* **3**, 19, 127–129.

Sharp, R.H. (1989) The price of success. Wilderness Odyssey, Sept./Oct., 32–34.

Sports Industry (1991) **88**, October.

Whiting, H.T.A. (1982) Skill in sport — A descriptive and prescriptive appraisal. In Salmela, J.H., Partington, J.T., & Orlick, T. (Eds.), New paths of sport learning and excellence. Ontario: *The Coaching Association of Canada.*

Chapter 6

LEARNING
AND THE INDIVIDUAL

We have dealt with many principles so far but little consideration has been given to the matter of individual differences and how methods might differ with particular groups such as the disabled, the young or expert performers. The need to consider the individual is highlighted in Sarsfield's (1973: p.5) comments in relation to diving instruction:

> It should be remembered that the whole personality of the individual is involved in acquiring the skill and that each person is unique. Each member of a class differs from the others in many ways: physically, intellectually and emotionally, and problems arising from these differences should be recognised. Furthermore, there is no best method of teaching a skill and no single way is right all the time; methods must be varied to suit the objective, the environment and the personalities of pupils and teacher.

The fact is we are all different in the way we perform, the things we like to do, the speed at which we learn, etc.. It seems likely therefore, that many of the topics in this book may not apply to all learners and others will apply with different degrees of emphasis. This chapter is an attempt to look at different categories of people, namely young/old learners and beginners/experts and specify which approaches are best suited to each one. A discussion such as this can not be definitive because of the subjectivity of categorising people. An attempt is made to guide the reader to those approaches which both the literature and anecdotal evidence tend to indicate are the favoured approaches for different groups of learners.

Working with youngsters

> Primary children are easily motivated and enjoy a variety of activities and stimulation. These attributes should excite any teacher of physical education. It is a matter of capturing this desire to be active and of structuring the learning environment to provide challenging, enjoyable athletic experiences.

This quotation from O'Neill (1991: p.5) reflects the importance most adults place on the value of movement, physical activity and sport for young children. In recent years, the subject of children and sport — especially competitive sport — has taken on a particular focus. Several agencies have set up working parties and many publications and conferences have tackled the many and varied concerns regarding sport and school age children. Issues such as early specialisation, training and overuse injuries, maximising of potential, competition, giftedness, etc., are just some of the topics investigated. Gleeson (1986) provides useful discussions of these and related matters. One topic asks what is the best way to teach youngsters? Are there particular techniques which are appropriate for more experienced learners? Should skills and sports be introduced at specific times?, and so on.

When to teach

A vast literature has examined the physical and performance standards of children of different ages — how fast can they run, how far can they jump, how far can they throw, etc. — (e.g., Shephard, 1982; Cratty, 1986; Lee, 1988). Investigators have debated concepts such as 'readiness' and 'critical periods' in learning. Other research has examined the merits of training children much earlier in their lives than would normally be expected, as well as the problems of depriving children of movement experiences.

There are many unanswered questions here as well as many generalisations. One thing which is clear is that children cannot be expected to learn a new activity unless their nervous system has matured sufficiently — they must be 'physiologically' capable. It would be wrong for example, to expect a three year old who has still to acquire a mature pattern of locomotion to learn a high hurdle technique, or to expect a four year old to catch a ball successfully. The progressive maturation of a child's physical and nervous make-up lays the foundation for increased learning in sports skills and this process cannot be speeded up. Only when the nervous system is 'ready' can learning occur.

The research does not tell us exactly when children are 'ready' to learn specific skills (Christina, 1975). One of the difficulties is that whilst children seem to mature in the same progressive manner, they do so at very different rates. In addition, timing the introduction of different sports varies from one sport to another. McNab (1986) suggests that with gymnastics four or five might be appropriate; swimming at seven or eight; soccer at nine or ten and athletics at ten to twelve. The sensitive coach or teacher who has the interests of the child close to heart should be able to judge fairly carefully what is the correct age and not make the mistake of starting too early.

What seems to be critical from the practitioner's perspective is how activities are presented and what form they take. With gymnastics for example, children as young as four could be introduced to a series of exploratory physical challenges which were stimulating and enjoyable. These would probably not bear much resemblance to the adult sport. Swimming at seven might be closer to the adult activity and include basic elements of stroke production. Soccer, might be a scaled-down version of the full game using grids. Athletics at pre-secondary school age would essentially be experiential rather than technical and only develop into well-defined activities related to the sport proper as the child grows. Traditionally, each sport has its own introductory techniques. The emergence of 'mini' sports has given this much more structure (e.g., Sleap, 1981; Towers, 1992)

Another way of interpreting the concept of 'readiness' is from a motivational point of view. Does the child want to learn? Is the child interested? What kinds of goals are available to strive for? It would seem more important to answer questions like this, because it doesn't matter how mature the learner may be, if he/she doesn't possess a desire to learn then he will not learn. The coach should therefore devote attention to making sure that everything is conducive to establishing the right attitude — safety, enjoyment, peer approval, reinforcement, etc..

Many people are of the view that during early childhood (up to five or six years of age) activity should be of a general physical nature and serve as a platform for later experience in specific sports. One school of child psychology underlines the importance of early movement experience as the basis for all development — including social, cognitive and motor dimensions. Paul Fitts (Fitts & Posner, 1967) considered that after the first few years of life, learning an entirely new skill is rare, all new skills being built out of already existing skills, and that the acquisition of skill is largely the transfer of prior habits to new situations. There is little hard scientific evidence to support this view and most data is empirical or anecdotal in nature.

If this assumption is true then one implication is that specific sports should not be introduced in early childhood but attention should be directed to modified or simplified versions. Thus, gymnastics might revolve around a general 'movement' training whilst many of the traditional team games and sports might lean towards the mini-sport approach (Sleap, 1981). This general strategy was adopted in a longitudinal project carried out in Glasgow (Pollatschek, 1987; 1989). In this study the intention was to examine the merits of daily physical education in the primary school. In the early primary years, pupil practice centred on basic ball handling and manipulative activities. Later, children were introduced to modified activities (e.g., 'king' ball) and then at the age of 10 years started mini sports. The project not only produced overwhelming support for daily PE, but it also supported the general to specific strategy for skill development. The secondary schools receiving the primary pupils involved in the project were forced to rethink the curriculum because the children were 'too skilled' for the existing programme of work!

Such an approach fits in well conceptually with the emphasis placed on young children and play. It is well known that early childhood is a period when the child likes to play, experiment and explore. Psychologists again suggest that it is through these means that the child comes to develop many expressive, intellectual, social and emotional abilities. It would make sense, then, to introduce new sporting activities within the context of play, reducing the number of rules, allowing freedom of individual pace and minimising situations which might create anxiety or fear. In addition, children might be allowed some freedom to make up rules and be encouraged to understand the objectives of movement/skills rather than acquire mastery of the techniques themselves. The transition from guided play to structured training is a matter for the individual coach or teacher; he/she must use intuition and experience to decide when the time is right to introduce new skills and to formalise procedures.

One early line of investigation examined the merits of special training designed to speed up skill acquisition (e.g., McGraw, 1935). This historical research, showed that improvements can be made but not to a level beyond normal. In other words, the benefit of introducing and developing skills before children are naturally ready shows no long term gain. Special training (as found in the Eastern bloc schools for sport — see for example, Riordan, 1986) only works if the child is physiologically ready. There is a suggestion that such training might enhance the child's self-confidence or bodily awareness but this is largely speculation. And there is the attendant danger that 'adult' skills taught too early may create technical problems later (McNab, 1986).

Other research has examined the notion of 'critical periods' for learning particular skills. Here, the suggestion is that if children are not exposed to certain skills before a certain age, then they will not be able to achieve full potential. Failure or difficulty on the part of a child to learn a given skill may arise because the child has passed the critical period for learning that skill. In relation to sports skills, the important experiments to answer these queries have not been undertaken (for ethical reasons). What can be said is that if early childhood is a time for acquiring basic movement skills which form a base for subsequent skill acquisition, then to maximise transfer childhood experiences should be as rich and varied as possible. This is the rationale behind commercial enterprises (e.g., 'Tumble Tots') which offer structured, intensive movement classes for children as young as two and three years.

Finally, with regard to the view that once a 'critical period' is passed, it is too late to start learning, it is worth reflecting on the ideas of Connolly (1969). He suggests that many cases where children experience difficulties in skill acquisition can probably be explained in terms of the efficiency of the teaching technique adopted, rather than the child not being 'ready' or able to learn. And it's also worth bearing in mind the number of adults introduced to sport (for recreation and competition purposes) who achieve high levels of skill.

Models for children

A common mistake is to treat children as small adults and impose techniques on them which are really only appropriate for adults. It would be wrong, for example, to expect a 10 year old to attempt a long jump using the hitch kick. This problem applies to many sports and can be extended to include the misuse of adult size equipment, playing areas and rules. How many readers can remember trying to swing an enormous tennis racquet or kick a soccer ball along a pitch which appeared miles long?. Problems like this can be resolved through the use of 'mini sports'. Mini sports are scaled down versions of the parent sport where equipment and playing areas are reduced in size, and play simplified, to enable children to grasp games more quickly and enjoy greater involvement. Because mini sports are based upon adult games, they emphasize all the basic skills and methods of play and are a very logical way of preparing young children for senior versions (Sleap, 1981).

Techniques which are right for the expert or adult may be totally inappropriate for the beginner. The sensitive coach should simplify or modify techniques so they 'fit' the age and skill level of the learner. He/she may even have to do away with 'good' technique altogether. McNab (1986) discusses this in relation to the kind and amount of information the child should be given. His ideas are described in Figure 16. In his model, there is information which the learner 'must' know, 'should' know and 'could' know. He gives the example of the long jump and a 15 year old beginner. McNab suggests the youngsters must know how to tackle an approach run in the 13-15 strides range, hitting the board accurately and landing with heels in line. They should know the means of holding speed into the take-off board, a vertical trunk and some attempt at lift. And they could know some sort of flight technique such as a hitch-kick or hang, and a longer, more structured, approach run. The problem for the coach is to put most of what he/she knows to one side and extract just the essence, using this to formulate a model for the children. With youngsters, the absolute basics are critical, for they are the pillars of future performance.

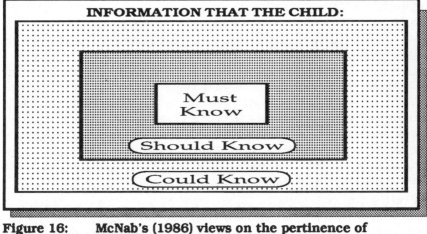

Figure 16:   **McNab's (1986) views on the pertinence of information input for children.**

Learning by imitation

The value of imitation has been underlined many times in this book. With children, imitation is an extremely strong force. It really is coaching on the cheap because there is so little for the coach to do except provide a good model. Anyone who watches children at play will note how readily they pick up the 'rules' and also how they mimic each other in their movements. An excerpt from McNab (1986: p.72) on teaching children golf is relevant here.

> In a very similar way, the child of eight or nine years can learn to play golf, or ski, or play most other sports, with far less difficulty than an adult pupil. The young child will immediately imitate with reasonable ease the movements he sees his teacher perform. He merely copies what he sees and is quite uninhibited by his initial failure. The child's approach to anything he sets out to learn shows a simplicity and delightful naivety which is sadly lost in the adult. The child just copies what he sees. He may need gentle words of encouragement occasionally, but as a rule the professional or parents appreciate that all they have to do is to show the child and the child will copy. The young child will watch the professional or parent and develop a kind of picture in his mind of the movements involved, slotting himself into this picture so that in his own mind he becomes the model he is copying.

The coaching of young children should take special advantage of this medium for learning, whether the coach demonstrates his own techniques, or another person — perhaps an older athlete — demonstrates, or a video/film is used.

The importance of movement

In general, children are restless and enjoy activity. Movement is an essential medium for normal, healthy development. Friendships, skills, values and many other things are developed as a by product of movement. Coaching or teaching approaches which keep children stationary soon lead to boredom and unrest on the part of the child. Sessions should be planned which are active and purposeful and which lead to challenge, co-operation with others and success (O'Neill, 1991).

Variety is also important. Children tend to have limited spans of attention which makes it impossible to sustain repetitive practice for long periods. Furthermore, it helps if children are not hampered by failure or negative transfer from unwanted skills. It is said that 'nothing succeeds like success', and children especially enjoy satisfaction from praise and reinforcement. The strength behind many proficiency award schemes lies in their capacity to challenge and reward with tangible outcomes.

It should be remembered however, that 'success is not the same as winning'. Practices which are geared to winning imply that some children will lose. The child who loses regularly will soon develop a low self-esteem.

Lee (1988) discusses in some detail the whole area of competitive sport and young children and in a recent statement (Lee, 1991: p.4) says:

> Perhaps the aim should be to concentrate a little less on competing strongly in childhood and a little more on nurturing the skills, enthusiasm and attributes which develop more effective adult competitors in the future.

Sensory vocabulary

Youngsters embarking on a new activity soon find out a lot more about their own body. Not only do they realise that muscles can ache, but they also begin to appreciate different ways in which their limbs can move or have to move. Consider for example, the feeling of heaviness experienced by a novice swimmer, the stretching of limbs felt by the gymnast or the imbalance felt by the young canoeist. This feel, or sensory awareness is obvious in some activities such as trampolining and diving but less obvious in others such as running or team games — though it may be equally critical. Why are these internal feelings important? For one thing they provide an effective medium for the coach and learner to communicate — a medium which can often compensate for the child's lack of technical knowledge and verbal skill. McNab (1986: p.70) expresses this very succinctly:

> This 'feel', this sensory awareness, relates not only to body or limb-positioning, but to limb-velocity and the balance of relaxation during movement. Once the athlete starts to 'read' his or her own body, he/she finds the acquisition of skill to be much less onerous. Equally important, he/she often comes back to the coach with his/her own vocabulary, own expression of movement, which can enrich both athlete and coach.

Such a 'movement' vocabulary (words such as strong, hard, effort, fast, etc.) are very meaningful to the learner and serve to describe how the learner feels without recourse to technical jargon. The coach can translate expressions like these into their technical equivalents and so discover the kinds of problems the learner is experiencing.

Safety and confidence

A strong feature of children's learning is the almost limitless confidence they display. For most children it is as if fear of injury or failure is completely absent. By and large, children have not developed the inhibitions, fears and bad habits which characterise adult learning. This allows the child, of course, to maximise his/her innate desire to learn and explore the surrounding world in the fullest way possible. Coupled with boundless energy, this makes for very rapid learning indeed. For the coach, however there is a dilemma. On the one hand there is a clear obligation to ensure the safety and well-being of those in his/her charge, whilst on the other hand the child's confidence provides him/her with the freedom to challenge the child beyond a point which many parents and onlookers would think safe or desirable. Again, the sensitive coach will decide — taking into account many other factors such as the goals set for the learner, and pressure from peers — how to balance these two competing tendencies.

Coaching style

Some research has shown that the 'approach' which coaches adopt can significantly determine the satisfaction children gain from sport as well as the likelihood they will drop out of the sport. Smoll and Smith (1979) have identified two clear approaches to coaching, one negative and the other positive. The positive approach encourages desirable performance by motivating children through positive feedback, praise and reward. The major force here is development of the learner's self-esteem. The negative approach relies on eliminating undesirable behaviours through negative feedback ("Don't do this"), criticism and punishment. The principal acting force here is rejection and fear. In their research, Smith and Smoll have found that the most important distinction between the coaches who children liked most and least is the amount of praise and reward used. Children enjoyed playing more in teams where coaches were positive, and they were more likely to continue in the sport if guided by 'positive' coaches. Children respond well to coaches who are open and friendly and they tend to repeat things which bring approval. It seems the best approach with children is one which is positive and encouraging. Lee (1988: pp.78/79) suggests that in order for children to get the best from their sport, the coach should be guided by three rules:

- Create a positive setting which encourages confidence and positive self-esteem.
- Make children aware that they can all succeed in their own terms — what really matters is the feeling associated with personal attainment rather than particular results.
- Create an enjoyable inter-personal atmosphere in which children are accepted by the coach and each other.

These and other issues are elaborated by Lee (1985; 1988), and Cratty (1986) provides an extremely comprehensive analysis of skill development in infants and young children.

Working with adults

Learning is something which continues throughout life and it doesn't stop when the child enters adulthood. It is usual for older people to take on new interests, (often into their 70/80s), indulge in different sports and tackle new skills. Children and adults do learn in different ways however. Adults usually learn more slowly than children. Often they are more fearful and sometimes less overtly enthusiastic. Physically, they may have severe limitations and may be less capable of adapting to change. However, adults have more experience than children and tend to tire or become bored less easily. Their powers of attention are also more capable. What are the implications for coaching of these and other factors?

Previous experience

If the view that new skills are built up from previously learned ones is true (Fitts & Posner, 1967; Connolly, 1977), then adults should possess a much richer and wider base on which to build new experiences. It has been suggested that adults are able to learn entirely new skills more easily than children when neither have any background in the specific area. Ausubel (1963) believes this is because adults can draw on transferable elements from past experience and apply them to the new situation, whereas youngsters lack this capacity. It is as if adults possess a greater repertoire of individual movement patterns (or subroutines to use the jargon of information processing theory) which can be adapted for new purposes. Adults are more 'streetwise'. The faster learning by adults assumes that all other things — motivation, fitness, etc. — are equal, but this, is not always the case. The reader will recall that transfer can be negative as well as positive. Sometimes adults display difficulty in picking up new skills because prior habits intrude, as happens, for example, when a different racket sport is learned or when an experienced swimmer tries to correct a faulty stroke pattern. A severe injury or accident can also have long-term negative effects and in such cases a period of uncertainty and interference often precedes solid gains in the new skill.

With this in mind, the interested coach or teacher should attempt to make some assessment of the adult's background (can they swim? which strokes can they do? how far can they swim? which is their best stroke? what other water sports do they do? etc.) in an attempt to find aspects which may transfer. Adult learners are good at recognising similarities and actively search for past learning on which they 'can hang their coat'. Advantage can be taken of this to speed up learning as well as help solve particular problems. In the case of potential negative transfer, the coach should highlight differences between previously learned skills and new ones (e.g., how does the flight of a badminton shuttle differ from that of a table tennis ball) so that new skills can be put into the right perspective.

Confidence

Adults generally display less confidence than children. Self-esteem is often a stumbling block and, because they are generally less mobile/fit, adults are exposed to a greater risk of injury. The good coach acknowledges these things in a number of ways. He/she might not be so demanding in his/her expectations; may work at a slower pace; may give more attention to physical warm up and certainly be more sympathetic to learning difficulties. Manual guidance as an appropriate technique might come more to the fore.

Cognitive ability

Research has shown quite clearly that up to the age of about 25 years, skilled performance increases. There is then a longish period during which there may be a gradual decline or, where experience and accuracy are important to success, progress may continue. However, after the age of about 25 years there is normally a progressive decline in just about every measurable aspect of skilled performance. Movement speed decreases, reaction time increases, anticipation worsens and so on (Welford, 1976). Also, as people get older, they find it increasingly difficult to comprehend or understand problems, especially when they are in any way new or unfamiliar or when a time stress is imposed. It seems that people just become slower with age. It has been suggested this reflects a slowing in neurological activity and possibly a more 'cautious' approach on the part of older learners (Schmidt, 1982). For the coach or teacher, the implications are the same as listed in the last section. He/she must be more tolerant and prepared to try several ways of approaching a problem, as well as more cautious in his/her expectations.

Finally, it should be said that many coaches find a number of advantages in working with adults over and above the pleasures of helping children. Coaching is a more sociable affair. Pressures on goal attainment and winning are lessened and adults are generally more reasonable and appreciative of the coach's efforts. Adults are more analytical and able to draw on their richer experience in order to solve new problems. Whilst this may not compensate for natural declines in fitness, speed, decision making etc., it aids communication with the coach and sometimes provides him or her with new ideas which can be explored with children. Adults are also more attentive, less distractable and usually prepared to apply themselves for longer periods to repetitive or seemingly trivial tasks.

Working with beginners

As people become more proficient skill changes in a number of ways. For example:

- There is a reduction in errors
- Bad habits are eliminated
- Movement becomes more efficient
- Accuracy, speed, timing, etc. improve
- Performance is more consistent
- The individual becomes more adaptable
- Performance is more automatic
- Individual 'style' becomes consolidated
- Self-analysis becomes possible
- Attention is more selective
- Irrelevant information becomes redundant
- Anticipatory awareness improves
- Confidence improves
- Technical knowledge becomes greater
- Goal direction becomes clearer, more realistic — etc., etc..

Note that some of these are observable and can be seen directly by the onlooker (increased speed, better timing) whilst most are intrinsic to the performer (self analysis, cue redundancy). If people do change in so many ways on their way to proficiency, then it would seem to follow that instructional methods used by the coach should take account of these changes.

Reducing the size of the problem

Fitts tells us — and most coaches would agree — that the initial problem with beginners is simply understanding the task ahead. To help, the coach must simplify matters by trying to extract the most important ingredients of the skill or game in question. It helps to reduce team games to small-side practices where the rules are few and involvement is maximal (e.g., mini sports). In closed skills such as trampolining, shaping or part techniques can be used to develop complex movements. For example, a somersault might begin with a forward roll on the trampoline bed. Skills must be reduced to manageable proportions but still retain their essential ingredients.

Beginners, especially youngsters may not possess a complete idea of the sport and know what it is all about. Videos shown briefly of experts in action or a question and answer session on rules, objectives, equipment, etc., can go a long way to helping the novice acquire an initial model.

Information selection

The learner is bombarded with information, most of which is irrelevant and distracting. The coach or teacher must search out the 'key' cues and attempt not to give too much feedback — often a frustrating exercise. The coach's ability to analyse performance and spot underlying causes of problems is critical, although at beginner level this will not present too much of a technical problem for the coach. To take a trampolining example once more, a beginner will display all manner of technical faults only one or two of which need to be identified. The learner might be told to concentrate on where to look, for example, and this would be reinforced over and over again. Frequently, the teacher or coach will find that directing attention to another fault will cause the learner to 'forget' the first one, which must be returned to fairly soon. Small, but important technical details soon become semi-automatic for the learner, although the coach must be vigilant. Repeating bad habits reinforces them; they must be curtailed early on.

A further way of reducing information load is to ensure that all competing sources of information are excluded. Is the sun shining in the learner's eyes? Can the coach be heard? Are other people distracting the learner? Does the learner feel safe? Does he/she know exactly what is required? Can questions be asked if the learner is unsure?, and so on. Highlighting cues visually (e.g., drawing hand/foot positions on the gymnastic mat, using brightly coloured balls and other pieces of equipment) helps focus the learner's attention.

The technique of 'hinting' (see Chapter 3) also helps the learner select the correct cues from amongst all other distracting features. A few examples illustrate this. With breast stroke leg action a flat foot position can be achieved by asking the learner to 'trap' a ball between his/her foot and shin. Telling the aspirant soccer player to dribble the ball as if it is attached to the shoe laces helps establish better control. Telling the skier to touch the ski tips with the knees helps develop good body posture, and suggesting to the trampolinist to bounce as if constrained by a narrow cardboard tube (a toilet roll!) sometimes helps improve technique and overall control.

Another technique used to help learners focus their attention is called 'verbalisation'. Many learners speak to themselves or sometimes aloud when they begin or carry out a movement. This seems to be a natural thing to do and fits in with Paul Fitts's idea that early learning is largely cognitive or intellectual in nature. The coach can help by providing the learner with a word or series of words to help focus on the important actions in a skill. For example, a trampolinist attempting a seat drop can say, "One, two, three and hips". For a somersault it might be, "One, two, three, hips and tuck". In squash, the learner trying to consolidate good backhand positioning when receiving the ball might say, "Face the side wall".

Presenting the model

For beginners, whether adults or children, imitation is an invaluable aid to learning. The coach often needs to say very little except draw attention to the salient cues (keep the ball for no longer than 5 seconds; keep your fingers closed; don't close your eyes). Learners can be directed to the point in question, shown the demonstration and then given the opportunity to practice. The use of one sense at a time (demonstrating and talking simultaneously divides the learner's attention) is critical. The coach or one of the group may demonstrate, or a video clip may be shown. In all cases, the model must be pitched at the correct level and illustrate the point in question. A world class hurdling action is no good for novices — for imitation to occur, the model must be attainable. In addition, the coach's model of 'correctness' must take account of individual differences such as weight, fitness, and gender.

Providing feedback

Learners often require a disproportionate amount of praise and feedback in relation to their level of skill. They have a weak basis for knowing whether or not they are correct — especially in activities where the form of the movement as opposed to its outcome, is important. The coach may be the only person who can monitor success. This means he/she must provide guidance and feedback on a regular basis — at least until the learner can begin to take over some of the analysis.

Feedback need not be especially specific in nature — technical perfection is not the goal in early learning. Furthermore, it should be couched in positive terms. Rather than say "No, your legs are in the wrong position altogether", the trampoline coach could say "Why don't you bring your legs together when in flight — feel your heels touch?". Fault finding and correction is a large portion of the coach/teacher's work. The chief difficulty is to keep it creative. It is all too easy to criticise without really helping people. Time spent deciding what/how to speak to the learner ensures that the coach or teacher's comments are not only informative but also encouraging. Beginners like to know they are getting better, and with beginners especially, the adage "success breeds success" is especially true.

If the coach thinks clearly about what he/she says to the learner, then the problem of simply describing errors should be avoided. The point was made in a previous chapter about the difference between describing errors and explaining their cause. The coach has to go a stage further and inform the learner how to correct the error. An example from gymnastics shows these steps. A common fault in a backward handspring (back flip) shows the gymnast landing on the feet but then falling forwards. One cause of this problem is insufficient backward rotation — the result of bending the arms on contact with the mat. All of this could be summarised by telling the gymnast to "lock your arms throughout the action". This way, the coach does not confuse the learner with unnecessary detail; it also translates the problem into a meaningful instruction which can be acted on by the learner.

Finally, the importance of providing feedback on a regular basis cannot be over-stressed. Beginners are as likely to learn correct actions as they are bad ones. If not halted early on, incorrect actions quickly become bad habits difficult to eradicate. The coach or teacher who is observant, attentive to all learners and who picks up faults as they arise should ensure that learning is always positive.

Practice considerations

Beginners tire easily because they lack specific fitness requirements and because they move inefficiently. The sensitive coach recognises that beginners cannot labour as long as the more experienced; he/she will also know that skill breaks down because of for example, limitations in fitness. Poor technique in bowling (cricket) may reflect gross shoulder inflexibility; in skiing, good technique will certainly be compromised through poor anaerobic conditioning. Practice should therefore be spaced or reduced accordingly.

Practice should be varied to stave off boredom and fatigue and as a way of appealing to different learners. Some people may prefer just to watch a demonstration and then 'have a go' whilst others may prefer an in-depth analysis before they begin. Different types and complexities of practice (e.g., 2 v 2; individual technical practices) ensures that people see the same thing from different perspectives and hence maximises the chances of all learning.

Beginners will make errors and some kinds of mistakes have positive benefits. Learning is much more meaningful if learners are given some responsibility for their own learning. Learners might be encouraged to assess why things have gone wrong or try out ideas which they think will solve particular problems. A problem-solving approach (e.g., in volleyball the coach could say— "why do you think the ball travels backwards every time you 'dig' it?") involves the learner in a positive way. It is also democratic. As an extension of this idea it may be profitable, in a group situation, to encourage learners to help each other with problems and feedback. Such a situation has to be treated with tact and sensitivity and will only work with learners who have some experience. Adult learners respond very well to this kind of approach.

Finally, practices must be seen by the learner to be relevant to the whole skill or game. What the coach perceives to be appropriate and what the learner sees as relevant, must be in agreement. If practice is isolated and non-game related, learners will vote with their feet and leave the sport or coach. The pressure is therefore on to devise practices which include the essentials of the game or sport proper. Beginner gymnasts for example, could — very early on — be introduced to some kind of competition (proficiency awards) or be taken by their coach to a local club event. Beginners in a team game such as volleyball can be initiated into the full game very quickly through the mini version.

Working with experts

A common misconception is that people who have become proficient (e.g., international athletes) have nothing else to learn. To give an example, most laypeople would say that gymnasts competing in the Olympic games couldn't get much better; they had reached a peak of excellence. Paradoxically, those same observers might still criticise the professional footballer and possibly even say they were better themselves, but that is another matter. The fact is that even athletes who are talented enough to represent their country may still have the potential to improve. Also, even experienced people are sometimes faced with new learning problems; they may become 'rusty' following a long lay-off; a new technique may appear or a new equipment design may demand an adjustment in technique (e.g., recent changes to the javelin and badminton racket). So what factors are important when working with people who are highly skilled?

Individual differences

At higher performance levels, no two people perform in exactly the same way. Techniques are, to a considerable degree, individualistic. Even in those sports where success is dictated by conformity to particular movement patterns (as for example, in gymnastics, and field athletics), people still display personalised forms of movement. The coach must work within the boundaries imposed by personal style. To try and alter it might cause long-lasting decrements in performance. For example, an international marathon runner whose running technique was examined using cine film was shown to have an asymmetrical arm action which sports scientists said was wasting energy. When his coach tried to make changes, the runner began to suffer sore legs and his performance fell away. To change a person's habitual way of performing in order to match a 'textbook' model, may take away the single quality which distinguishes the athlete from all the rest!

Attentional capacity

The expert performs 'on automatic pilot'. Unlike the novice, he/she does not have to consciously think through every movement, but can confine his/her conscious thought to matters to more cognitive activities such as decision making and perception, leaving the movements to 'take care of themselves'. This freeing of attention makes it possible for the expert to work on aspects of performance which are irrelevant earlier in learning or else too subtle for the novice to appreciate. In climbing for example, experts are especially interested in practising techniques for protecting themselves as they ascend the rock. In addition, they come to appreciate how differences in rock texture and type influence the kinds of holds available and hence the hand/foot actions necessary for safe movement. In badminton, the expert will understand that to play successfully at international level, a knowledge of different footwork patterns, and how each relates to the kinds of strokes possible, is essential.

This means that the coach can help the athlete on fine technical/ tactical matters which are not appropriate earlier on. It also means the coach can work with the player as he/she performs without causing significant loss in performance. Coaching from the sideline — whilst the player is performing — therefore becomes a viable method.

The coach can help in other ways too. Because skilled performance is largely automatic, it means the performer is often unaware of exactly how he/she performs particular skills. The expert can become unaware of his/her movements *per se* and tend to concentrate only on the outcome of those movements (did the shuttle land in court?, was the somersault spotted correctly?, how far was the javelin thrown?, etc.). In this way, faulty technique can creep in and lay the foundations for bad habits unless an outsider detects the error. There is a need therefore for vigilance on the part of the coach in detecting small changes in technique which may go unnoticed by the athlete. There is a problem here however. Forcing an expert to attend to muscular feelings and movements may well inhibit the action of unconscious cues that are necessary for controlled movement ('paralysis from analysis'!). Asking the performer to step back to an earlier stage in the learning process may well disturb performance dramatically. However, this may be the penalty which has to be paid for improving the athlete's ultimate level of performance. It demonstrates a phenomenon which is known as the 'progression-regression' hypothesis:

under unfavourable conditions — such as stress — the performer reverts to an earlier level of control and skill suffers accordingly (Fuchs, 1962).

Practice conditions

If the 'whole' method is preferable with novices, then with experts — who are well motivated and understand what they are trying to do — part practices are more meaningful and in fact, highly desirable. As the learner progresses, it follows that techniques become more specialised and so practices too, should become more specialised. In addition, practice may need to be highly individualistic. For example, think of the practices which a gymnast and her coach must devise to develop a specific, complicated asymmetric bar routine in gymnastics.

If practice is more specific then the terminology used by the coach will also be more specialised. The skilled performer possesses a much richer vocabulary than the beginner for understanding and communicating with the coach. Instructions such as "shorten/lengthen your backswing", "keep a wide base", are much more meaningful to the expert performer, which makes it possible for the coach and performer to work together on specific game aspects at a level which may be quite inaccessible to the novice.

Skilled athletes are more capable of listening to detailed instructions, better disposed to sitting down with the coach and analysing problems, and better able to appraise their performance without the immediate help of the coach. Experts can often profit from self-analysis (e.g., watching videos of their performance) and experiment with technique without guidance, their greater experience and sensitivity to what their body is doing permitting them to make adjustments without external feedback.

Mental rehearsal

Mental rehearsal is discussed in detail in Chapter 7, but is mentioned here because of its particular relevance to experts. It has been argued for many years that mental rehearsal is an essential part of the elite athlete's preparation for competition (Ryan, 1981; Rushall, 1979). It helps prepare the body and mind for competition and also serves as an important tool in maintaining concentration and attention. Its use is well documented and many outstanding performers from sports as diverse as skiing, golf, lawn tennis and weight-lifting testify to its value. As well as an aid to competition, mental rehearsal has also been shown to act as a learning aid and improve performance, especially with elite or highly skilled individuals. The reasons would seem to be two-fold. In the first place, skilled performers possess a model of skill which is conceptually better established than that of learners, so consequently, mental rehearsal should have a greater effect with experts because it is has a sound basis. Secondly, experts are not concerned with the generalities of their sport; their training is highly specific, their goals are clearer, and they are often searching for ways to extract just that little bit more from themselves.

They have an attitude which is more conducive to mental rehearsal.

In practice, it is likely that skilled performers — especially those who are highly motivated — spend a substantial amount of time thinking about their sport, and a significant proportion of this time will be structured as mental rehearsal both on and off the field. Mental practice is an acquired activity however and the athlete needs to learn how to do it. Sport psychologists suggest that mental rehearsal should be built into an athlete's training programme.

One of the problems of mental rehearsal is that it takes time — time which the athlete may wish to devote to more practical endeavours. In addition, it is very susceptible to interference from problems which may occupy the athlete's attention (e.g., personal matters, injury). It therefore requires practice and self-evaluation by the athlete as well as monitoring by the coach to be effective. Its timing must also be appropriate.

Summary

1. Many studies have examined the performance standards of children at different ages, but there is little research evidence to show when are the most appropriate times for introducing different sports to children.

2. Children must be physiologically mature before they will learn particular skills.

3. Childhood is a 'skill hungry' stage; children apparently enjoy activity for its own sake, they are motivated to learn and they readily acquire many basic movement patterns. It is suggested that beyond the age of 5 or 6 years, children rarely acquire entirely new skills.

4. Many sports can be introduced through a form of structured play. Mini sports are especially useful.

5. The research on critical periods in learning and special training has thrown little light on skill development.

6. Techniques for children should not be as sophisticated as those for adults, and they should also be adapted to suit the size and shape of the individual.

7. Visual guidance should take advantage of imitation and verbal guidance should acknowledge the child's limited technical vocabulary.

8. Safety and confidence are critical considerations with youngsters, as is coaching style. Research shows that positive methods are more likely to produce positive results than negative ones.

9. Adult learners are able to take advantage of greater experience when learning new sports. The rapid learning which is sometimes found represents the presence of positive transfer.

10. Adults may be intrinsically more motivated to learn and are often more analytical in their approach.

11. Fear of injury and lack of confidence may impede the learning of adults.

12. Teaching beginners has a number of implications for coaching/ teaching — skills should be reduced in their information content; relevant cues should be selected; feedback should not be too technical and should be provided regularly; practice should not tire the learner; practice should be varied, interesting and relevant.
13. Most experts have the potential to improve and are often faced with new learning problems.
14. Experts should be treated as individuals in the way they are coached. Technical proficiency, 'style', fitness requirements, etc., are very personal at high levels of skill.
15. Experts are able to respond to highly specific outside advice, often when performing. They are also more able to self-assess their performances.

Discussion questions

1. Take a situation where you introduce a new skill to a youngster, say a forward roll or striking a tennis ball. Suppose the youngster fails to pick up the idea. What are the possible causes of failure? How would you examine the precise problem?
2. Youngsters can be very noisy and undisciplined. What steps can be taken to attract their attention to the sport/skills in question?
3. Think of an example from your experience which demonstrates the principle that models for children should accommodate their shape, size, and so on.
4. Children can imitate both good and bad technique and they may do so with equal success. How would you know whether the child's poor technique was a result of their inability or your own faulty demonstration?
5. Children invent games by themselves and in conjunction with others devise rules for playing the game. Examine some of the problems for a teacher/coach in trying to use this natural process as a means of introducing popular sports.
6. Children are, by and large, very confident. What do you think of the view that children often put themselves at too great a risk to life and limb?
7. Research shows that positive coaching styles are superior in their effect to negative ones. With this in mind, how sensitive/tactful should the coach be when describing errors to children?
8. Describe an example from your experience to show that adult learners can be very analytical in their approach to learning.
9. To what extent can a coach take advantage of an adults past experience when introducing a new skill?
10. What steps can be taken to overcome the problems of fear and injury when working with adults?
11. Take a particular sport and describe the cues which would be highlighted to a beginner (say, in the first session).

12. If expert performers have the potential to improve even further, what steps can be taken to ensure this does happen?
13. Comment on the situation where experts are encouraged to practice a technique beyond the point of their physical ability and to a level where skill begins to break down.

References

Ausubel, D.P. (1963) *The psychology of meaningful verbal learning.* New York: Grune & Stratton.

Christina, R.W. (1975) What research tells the practitioner about children's motor development. Paper presented to the AAHPER Convention, Atlantic City, New Jersey, March.

Connolly, K. (Ed.) (1969) *Mechanisms of motor skill development.* New York: Academic Press.

Connolly, K. (1977) The nature of motor skill development. *Journal of Human Movement Studies,* **3**, 128–143.

Cratty, B.J. (1986) *Perceptual and motor development in infants and children (3rd. ed.).* Englewood Cliffs, New Jersey: Prentice Hall.

Fitts, P.M. and Posner, M.I. (1967) *Human performance.* Belmont, Calif.: Brooks/Cole.

Fuchs, A.H. (1962) The progression-regression hypothesis in perceptual-motor skill learning. *Journal of Experimental Psychology,* **63**, 177–182.

Gleeson, G. (Ed.) (1986) *The growing child in competitive sport.* Hodder & Stoughton: London.

Lee, M. (1985) The importance of positive relationships. *Coaching Focus,* **2**, Autumn, 1985.

Lee, M. (1988) *Coaching Children (NCF key course resource pack).* National Coaching Foundation: Leeds.

Lee. M. (1991) Coaching children. *Coaching Focus,* **16**, 3–5.

McGraw, M.B. (1935) *Growth: A study of Johnny and Jimmy.* New York: Appleton-Century-Crofts.

McNab, T. (1986) Technique and the young performer. In Gleeson, G. (Ed.) *The growing child and competitive sport.* Hodder & Stoughton: London.

O'Neill, J. (1991) Teaching athletics in the primary school. *British Journal of Physical Education,* **22**, 3, 5–6.

Pollatschek, J.L. (1989) Daily physical education in Scotland. Submitted to *Canadian Association for Physical Education, Health and Recreation.*

Pollatschek, J.L. (1987) The psycho-physical effects of daily physical education on pre-adolescent children. Doctoral dissertation, University of Strathclyde, Scotland.

Riordan, J. (1987) Talent spotting, ability levels and progress in Eastern Europe. *Coaching Focus*, **5**, Spring.

Rushall, B.S. (1979) *Psyching in sport*. London: Pelham Books Ltd.

Ryan, F. (1981) *Sports and psychology*. Englewood Cliffs, N.J.: Prentice Hall Inc.

Sarsfield, N.W. (1973) *Diving instruction*. EP Publishing Ltd.: Wakefield.

Schmidt, R.A. (1982) *Motor control and learning*. Champaign, Illinois: Human Kinetics Publishers.

Shephard, R.J. (1982) *Physical activity and growth*. London: Year Book Medical Publishers.

Sleap, M. (1981) *Mini sport*. Heinemann Educational Books: London.

Smoll, F.L. and Smith, R.E. (1979) *Improving relationship skills in youth sport coaches*. East Lansing, MI: Institute For The Study Of Youth Sports.

Towers, C. (1992) Mini-Tennis and racquet type. Unpublished M.Phil. Thesis, Jordanhill College, Glasgow.

Welford, A.T. (1976) *Perceptual and motor skills*. Glenview, Illinois: Scott Foresman.

Chapter 7

MIND OVER MATTER

Introduction
The title of this chapter is a much-used cliché which hints at one of the major problems that has dogged sports coaching and teaching for many years, i.e., the unnecessary distinction which is often made between the learner's thoughts and feelings (the 'mind') and the learner's skills and movements (the 'matter'). Rintala (1991) has recently reviewed the philosophical history of the mind-body dualism pointing to the tradition of dualisms and dichotomies of western civilisation. He argues strongly for a much more integrated understanding of teaching.

Historically, researchers and practitioners have placed emphasis on the technicalities and content of learning — techniques, how they should be broken down, how long they should be practised for, and so on. The learner has often been ignored at the expense of over-attention to technique, movement and the 'output' side of the learning process. More recently the focus has rapidly changed and the 'psychology' of the individual has taken on a much more important role. Matthews (1991), for example, discusses the important role of the sports psychologist in helping athletes to overcome a number of problems such as how to relax and reduce tension and how to build confidence and self-belief. Hardy (1990) has stressed the importance of psychological parameters as they affect performance and Byrne (1986) has also focused on these important developments in a recent publication appropriately referred to as 'The athlete's mind — the last frontier'. Hardy (1986) refers mainly to the competitive situation although many of his points are relevant to the learner. He says (p.2):

> Looking at the preparation of the few world class performers that Britain has produced helps to establish what some of these psychological factors might be. By linking this evidence to the research into the psychological phenomena of peak performance, we can make some educated guesses about what the factors are that we need to bring under control. These include goal-setting, self-confidence, persistence, concentration, relaxation, activation and anxiety.

The Cognitive approach to learning (see Chapter 1) gives credence to people's perceptions and goals and the influence of these factors on behaviour. Instances are seen in sport all the time. Take for example, the middle distance runner who fails because of over-anxiety, or the tennis player who prepares by mentally rehearsing movements over and over just before performance. Numerous top performers testify to the value of mental training. For example, Billy Jean King applied mental strategies not only to rehearse strokes and tactics to 'groove' good technique, but she also rehearsed moments of victory to enhance her confidence and motivation (Jones, 1974).

The fact is that learners are not machines. Feelings, attitudes and expectancies should not be ignored. It has been shown that these factors and others are important forces which determine not only the speed with which skill is acquired and the level of ultimate success, but also the amount of enjoyment experienced by the learner and the length of time he/she continues in sport. These variables are relevant to beginners and experts as well as young and older students of learning. The objective in this chapter is to take a look at some of these issues which have particular relevance to learning. The 'Inner Game' is one approach to teaching/coaching and learning which brings together a number of important ideas.

The Inner Game

The inner game approach to coaching and learning views the learner's mind, learning and movements as a whole. It is concerned with the manner in which the coach or teacher approaches skill problems — the 'coaching style' — as well as the way in which the learner is involved in the learning process. It addresses both the physical and mental components in sport. It is also an approach which the learner can use for self-instruction. Tim Gallway (e.g., Gallway & Kriegal, 1977) coined the expression 'Inner Game' and introduced the subject some 15 years ago, but his idea is not especially novel (p.6):

> The Inner Game approach is hardly new. It is similar to the natural way that, as children, we learned to walk, talk or throw a ball. It uses the unconscious, rather than the deliberately self-conscious mind. This process doesn't have to be learned; we already know it. All that is needed is to unlearn the habits and concepts which interfere with our natural learning ability, and to trust the innate intelligence of our bodies.

Gallway draws on several learning theories, but notably the Cognitive and the Information-processing models. Let us explore the approach in more detail. Gallway argues that traditional coaching and teaching methods have a number of inefficient and negative dimensions. Firstly, traditional methods are too technically oriented and create barriers between learner and instructor. Crimble (1982: p.1) expresses this view in the following:

> Could it be that as teachers and students we are in love with the tech-nicalities and jargon of our sport? If the skill is made to appear too simple it undermines our position of authority and denigrates our efforts to master it. A convenient smoke-screen of technicalities reinforces our ego and provides an excuse for our failures.

Gallway argues that a technical orientation focuses the learner's attention on the results of actions rather than the feelings of movements. This presents an obstacle to improvement because the learner is pre-occupied with self-analysis and self-appraisal and is, therefore, constantly pre-occupied with failure. A knock-on effect is that fear of failure provides a further obstacle to positive achievement. Gallway goes on to suggest that because of an over emphasis on performance-oriented coaching/learning, learners lose interest and cease enjoying sport. Finally, he argues that focusing on performance success/failure, encourages aggressive self-instruction and self-criticism, which leads to anxiety and tension inhibiting the learning process. In addition, the muscular tension created through over-anxiety inhibits technical excellence.

Gallway attempts to encourage a much more positive approach where the learner is not only centrally involved with his/her own learning, but is also 'de-tuned' to the ideas of success and failure. A major premise is that learners have a potential to succeed and possess inherent talents well beyond their expectations. He bases this partly on the finding that sometimes people display 'highs', i.e., occasions when they display high technical excellence with no lapse in attention and total enjoyment. He gives an example from the world of skiing (p.17):

> All of us have had those incredible runs when for some reason everything seems to click and we ski so much better than usual that we surprise ourselves. Turns we've been struggling with are suddenly easy. Frustrations vanish and we become totally absorbed in the joy of the moment. The usual mental struggle — trying to do everything right, worrying about how we look or about falling and failing — is forgotten. Enjoyment is so intense that we don't even think of making a mistake — and we don't. For a time, self-imposed limitations are forgotten; we are skiing unconsciously.

Gallway suggests that we all possess the ability to perform 'out of our mind', but we don't do it because we build barriers which interfere with the normal mechanisms for success. The release of potential is brought about by an alteration in the state of our mind, i.e., when we stop thinking. He says (p.19):

> We can only conclude that the reason we don't perform so well is not that we don't have the ability, but that we somehow interfere with it. In the breakthrough run we skied beyond our expectations not because we finally mastered a new technique but because for a few moments our state of mind changed. The mind became quiet, making our movements more natural and coordinated. Such occasions indicate that the excellence of our skiing is dependent more on our state of mind than on the self-conscious mastery of memorised techniques.

To help clarify these ideas Gallway distinguishes between two hypothetical learners — 'Self 1 and Self 2'. Self 1 is the person within the learner who does the talking, judging, worrying and doubting. Self 1 creates self-concepts and fears and is normally in control. Self 2 is the person being instructed who performs the actions. Self 2 has the potential to respond with full capability but is thwarted by the barriers erected by Self 1. Gallway argues that in most cases Self 1 and Self 2 don't get along too well; they 'mistrust' one another and behave as two separate persons. The exception is during childhood when Self 1 has not had time to accumulate distorted and limiting self-concepts. This allows Self 2 the freedom to learn and perform in a natural and confident manner. With adult learners the position is different and conflict exists. The major object is to quieten Self 1 and so free the obstacles which otherwise prevent Self 2's fullest expression and development.

How does this theory help us to ensure that learners achieve their potential ? How is it possible to minimise interference caused by Self 1?

Trust and confidence

Gallway suggests that learners can begin to realise their potential and to enjoy learning much more by 'taming' Self 1 and 'trusting' Self 2. Recognising the existence of Self 1 and its damaging effects is a start to reducing its effect. Beginning to trust the body and develop confidence is a start to enhancing the efforts of Self 2. What can the coach do to help here? Trying to reduce the learner's anxiety helps. By eliminating criticism, listening to learners, respecting their feelings and ideas and generally treating them as partners in a mutual adventure goes a long way to reducing anxiety. Ensuring a safe environment and making instructions simple and brief obviously gives support. Confidence and self-image can be improved by giving the learner maximum responsibility for his/her learning. This may require a different style of coaching — one which is more sympathetic and forgiving — to that which the coach normally adopts. Overall, coaching and teaching should ensure that learners believe in their skill levels and it should aim to minimise the verbal badgering and self-condemnation for mistakes which are often the hallmark of the learning period (Matthews, 1991).

Body awareness

To increase the learner's confidence and belief in what is possible it is essential to give Self 2 a higher profile. To do this Gallway accepts the notion of 'experiential learning' or 'learning by doing'. 'Thinking about doing' is taboo. He says (p.39):

> Self 2 lets experience be the guide. Remaining objective and interested, it grows by absorbing what is happening from moment to moment. In the process of discovery it senses and observes, constantly picking up information and making appropriate adjustments in its actions and direction, thus becoming increasingly able to cope with the situation at hand. The natural learning process is discovery by experience.

The essence of this approach is feedback. Feedback of all kinds is useful, but feedback from internal sensations is critical. It is through internal feedback that body awareness increases, which in turn brings Self 2 to the fore. Gallway suggests the way to help the learner increase body awareness is to make him/her responsible for his/her actions and thus force attention to sensations which might otherwise be ignored. Through being told less what to do and feeling more what is going on in the body, the learner becomes attuned to results and more to the muscular feelings associated with body technique. He gives an example of a coach introducing beginner skiers to the notion of 'edge' control. The learners are asked to get used to their skis by shifting their weight from foot to foot, moving them up and down and sideways, and so on. The coach then tells them to follow him/her up the hill, but does not mention anything about edge technique. The coach simply talks to the group, asking them to feel their skis and asking whether they feel flat or inclined. After a short while the group is asked to 'play' with different degrees of edge and see what happens. The learners go through a process of flattening their skis, slipping and correcting. In this way, each learner gains control and increased sensitivity entirely through his/her own efforts. Gallway argues this goes a long way to helping the learner gain confidence and awareness, which in turn allows the potential of Self 2 to be realised.

In another example, Gallway shows how the learner can become sensitized to internal feedback. In this example, a tennis coach tries to correct a bad serving technique in which the learner hits too hard. The coach tells the player to serve the ball as hard as possible, but to ignore where it lands, and to give the effort felt in the arms a score of 10. The player is then asked to serve a soft ball which is given a 1. The player is then asked to serve the ball with varying degrees of effort and to give scores from 1 to 10. The net result is that the learner becomes proficient in hitting the ball with less effort, and is able to do so because he/she is more aware of what the body is saying.

The Inner Game approach to teaching and learning presents nothing new and is a good example of theory and practice meeting in a common aim. Its basic principals are sound and it most definitely supports the recent interest in the "games for understanding" approach to games teaching.

On a negative note, it is important to say that it has not attained wide publicity or acceptance — possibly because it has not been taught correctly or is perceived as too difficult to understand (Fisher, 1991). Despite this, Inner Game proponents attempt to elicit the very best from learners, try to eradicate some of the common hurdles to success such as fear of failure by switching the responsibility for learning from coach to learner, and attempt to make learners more aware of what their bodies are doing and 'saying'. All of these are summed up in a final quotation from Gallway and Kreigal (1977: p.111):

Learning happens best when both instructor and student recognise that experience is the teacher. The role of the instructor is to guide the student into experiences appropriate to his stage of development. At the same time that the student is guided towards attentive appreciation of the sensations of his body, the instructor is learning from him how to best lead him to the next step.

Goal setting strategies

In the Chapter 1, skill was defined and one of the important criteria listed was goal-direction. Skill has purpose and direction. For example, a diver completes a complicated routine aimed at entering the water in a vertical position, and a soccer player attempts to dribble the ball past an opposing defender to move closer to the goal posts. The performer's intentions in situations like these are usually well defined and easily seen by the observer. But goal direction is not just important in skilled performance. For the learner too, targets must be established in order for progress to continue in a structured and successful manner. Goal setting — the process of establishing appropriate goals — has a number of important criteria which are worth examination.

The need for goals

One of the important determiners of success in sport is self-confidence. A person who is self-assured and aware of his/her full potential is more likely to succeed than someone who is unsure and lacks confidence. It has been shown for example, that performers who believe they have the ability to achieve, achieve more and are more persistent in the event of failure than less confident performers (Schubert, 1985). There are a number of factors involved in helping to build confidence, but the most effective way is to ensure that learners succeed in their efforts. The only way this can happen is for learners to strive towards goals at which they can succeed. The setting of realistic and attainable goals — by the learner and coach — provides a yardstick against which the learner can measure his/her own performance. And if major goals can be broken into lesser targets, then success occurs throughout learning. The cycle of events shown in Figure 17 is a model which applies to all sporting endeavours.

There is another reason why goal setting is crucial. Setting goals allows coaches and athletes to plan the direction in which they are heading and the best route taken to get there. A well-thought out training plan involving weekly and monthly targets is more likely to result in success than a 'hotch-potch' of ill-conceived ideas left hanging in the air. A carefully designed programme of major and secondary goals provides the basis for structured training — amount, nature, timing, etc. — and makes for efficient use of time and resources. In addition, because goal setting involves establishing specific criteria or targets, it is possible to measure and evaluate the learner's progress in a concrete manner.

Evaluation of the learner therefore takes on a much more meaningful dimension and has a sounder basis. Evaluation is discussed more fully in Chapter 8.

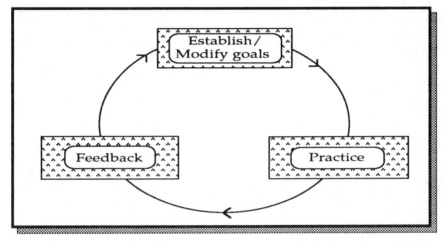

Figure 17:   A simple scheme showing the link between goals, action and feedback.

Long and short-term goals

If goals are to be effective, they must be specific to the learner and the situation but, they must also lie within the learner's control. For example, it would be inappropriate for a good club table tennis player to set the goal of becoming, say, national champion. Such a goal would not only be too far away in time (it might be a good long-term goal), but it is also influenced by the skill of other performers. It makes sense to establish goals which can be achieved in the long term, but also to set intermediate goals which are manageable and attainable in the short term. A very detailed example of how long-term intentions can be broken down into smaller goals is seen in the efforts of an international swimmer who wished to win a gold medal at the 1976 Olympics. The swimmer calculated from previous times what performance time might win the gold, and determined that he had to drop four seconds in four years. He then broke the goal down further into one second per year, one tenth of a second per month, one three-hundredth of a second per day, and one twelve hundredth of a second per hour of training! Finally, he made this goal of one twelve-hundredth of a second per hour a little easier to grasp by working out that from the time he began to blink his eyes to the time his eyelids touched was five twelve-hundredths of a second. This was a target he could reach in one hour, and so he set about doing just that. His plan worked and he won the gold medal to prove it.

Mutrie (1985) shows how long-term or so-called 'dream' goals can be broken down into smaller parts. Figure 18 shows this approach.

In the top section of Figure 18, the lowest step represents the learner's current level of performance and the highest step represents the learner's overall goal. The difference has been broken into a number of intermediate goals which help make the long-term goal more achievable. The bottom section of Figure 18 shows in turn how the steps between the intermediate goals are further divided by short-term goals which are specific and attainable targets. Mutrie makes the point that models like this must be flexible enough to account for unexpected problems (e.g., injuries, eradication of bad habits).

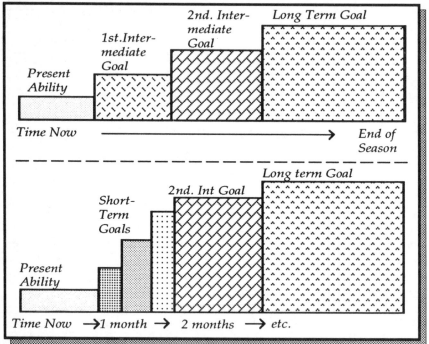

Figure 18: Schematic view to illustrate how goals can be sub-divided into short-term goals. Based on Mutrie (1985).

Hardy and Fazey (1986) present a similar, tree-like structure to goal-setting. They suggest the coach and learner should work together to establish a set of, say, three long-term aims which are realistic and measurable in quantitative terms. Next, they should be ranked in order of importance. For the most important aim a list of goals which can be attained within a month and which contribute to the achievement of the overall aim should be written down and also ranked. For the second long-term aim, one goal should be established which can be attained within a month. Nothing is established for the final long-term aim. Now, for the first monthly goal corresponding to the first aim three sub-goals or courses of action should be devised which can be met within a week. For the second monthly goal, two intermediate goals are selected. And so on.

Table 2 shows this scheme applied to a gymnast working towards team selection for a national squad.

Table 2: A specific example showing how long-term goals are broken down into medium-term goals which, in turn are divided into specific courses of action. This is an example of multiple goal-setting for a male gymnast decided by the gymnast, together with his coach, following a discussion of the previous season's progress.

LONG-TERM AIM	GOALS FOR THE NEXT MONTH	GOALS AND COURSES OF ACTION FOR THIS WEEK
	1. Learn one new move on each of side horse (Stockli B), parallel bars (cast half-turn to support), high bar (Stalder)	1.1 Learn straddle circle on low bar 1.2 Start work on Stockli B and cast half-turn (at least two half-hour sessions on each during the week) 1.3 Do not give in if success is not immediate
A. Learn the new World Set routines	2. Learn the correct sequencing of all the set routines using mental rehearsal	2.1 Send away for the latest FIG interpretation of the set routines 2.2 Mentally rehearse the four conventional routines at home for 20 minutes each day
	3. Link three moves together from each routine	
B. Score 49.0 on voluntary routines	4. Maintain present performance on all voluntary routines	4.1 Practise full voluntary routines in two halves if necessary on the floor, vault and rings
C. Win a place in the British Men's Squad		

What Table 2 shows is a hierarchy of aims and goals indicating items of greater or lesser importance. It is important to note an aspect which Mutrie also mentions which is that the model must be seen as a dynamic one which grows and changes over time. In the above example the learner and coach would evaluate success in terms of goal-attainment, re-evaluate monthly goals and set new goals for the following week. So, every week some aims would leave, new ones would appear and others would alter in their importance. It is also important to notice that specific goals need not be skill-oriented. It may be equally valid for the learner to complete a training diary, purchase new equipment or perhaps spectate at a competition. These might be 'easy' goals to attain and help balance more arduous ones.

Criteria for good goals

Most authorities agree that goal setting should be a joint plan between the learner and the coach. This is especially true with advanced learners who are more experienced and better able to participate in informed discussion. Goals established in this way are more likely to meet a number of important criteria.

It goes almost without saying that goals must be specific and tailored to suit the individual. Goals which are not specific are likely to cause confusion and lack of direction in the learner's mind. Goals can be derived from the learner's current problems. For example, suppose a tennis player cannot execute backhand strokes consistently. This could be converted into a positive statement such as — "Over the next two months, I will improve my backhand by spending half an hour each day on good technique". It is vital the learner expresses negative thoughts and actions as specific, positive goals.

Goals should also be appropriate to each learner. People learn at individual rates and are motivated in different ways. One person may be able to learn a new gymnastic move in a single session whilst another may require several weeks. A good coach/teacher will know exactly how far to push each individual and know what to expect in a given amount of time.

Goals should be challenging. Targets which are too easy to attain or limited in scope run the risk of de-motivating the learner. People are more likely to persist when faced with a challenge which presents problems but which is not too demanding or impossible. Again, a sensitive coach should know his/her athletes well enough to determine what is appropriate in any given situation.

Goals must also be attainable. Targets which cannot be met in the time allowed or are just impossible to meet, will force learners into failure situations and similarly de-motivate. Hardy (1986) throws some light on this matter in his examination of the relationship between goal difficulty ('attainability') and performance. He suggests that for goals which are under the individual's own control, there is an inverted-U relation between the goal difficulty and performance (see Figure 19) such that performance increases up to a critical point and then drops away.

The critical point marks the stage at which the individual ceases to accept the goal as attainable. The exact value of the critical point depends on a number of situational influences (e.g., competition, type of sport) and subjective factors (e.g., anxiety, personality), but Hardy indicates that as a rough guideline, goals in practice should be at least 50% achievable. This would seem to be intuitively correct.

Goals must be realistic in the sense that they relate to the overall goals the coach or teacher has in mind. In the swimming example given before, the performer established target times which he considered were attainable. They were also logical steps towards the final time required, i.e., they were realistic. A problem arises when intermediate goals are unattainable or don't fit into the overall pattern of skill development. For example, a gymnastics coach may expect a beginner to learn a movement which requires too much strength, is too complicated or not seen by the learner to relate to the sequence being learned. This raises the problem that sometimes when goals are not achieved, the coach must determine whether failure is due to the learner or the coach.

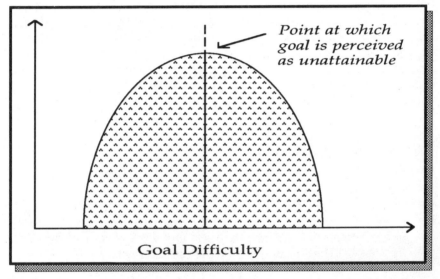

Figure 19: **Hypothetical relationship between goal difficulty and performance.**

Goals must be measurable. The whole process of goal setting breaks down if neither learner or coach can confirm whether goals have been attained. To help, it makes sense to establish goals which are objective and quantifiable. Measures of time and distance for example, are far better than subjective terms like, 'more', 'enough', 'better', and so on. A number of measurement techniques are available and include the use of recognised skill tests (number of free shots out of 20; proficiency award schemes) and match analysis methods which are particularly appropriate in team sports. One of the difficulties with measurement is that it is easier to concentrate on the 'outcome' of performance than the performance itself (e.g., number of baskets scored as opposed to the quality of the shot). This leads the learner to focusing on aspects of performance which are related to the overall goal but not intermediate ones. For example, the beginner swimmer who tries to swim a width of the pool unaided (a very play very poor technique and possibly start to develop a bad habit. Somehow, the overall goal to swim unaided has to be broken down into smaller parts which are measurable but which also focus on technique. Use of 'number of strokes' might be a way around this problem.

Mutrie (1985) discusses this problem by suggesting that 'product' goals which relate to the outcome of performance should be used for long-term targets, whilst 'process' goals which refer to the process of improving performance towards the ultimate target, should be set for intermediate or short-term goals. Her reasoning here is that product goals (e.g., to be the national champion), whilst giving direction to a general plan of action, are inappropriate for short-term application because they tend to be influenced by outside factors (e.g., the performance of other people). It is far better in the short-term to set goals which can be controlled by the learner and which refer specifically to the learner's own performance.

Finally, it is critical that goals are written down on paper. The learner may keep a diary and/or the coach might maintain a log of everyone's progress and targets. In this way, it is clear to everyone what is required whilst reviews and evaluation become more objective.

Mental Rehearsal

Find a few minutes and a quiet place to lie down. Imagine the mountains: a specific mountain on a fine, crisp, winter's day. Imagine yourself stepping out of the cable car, or getting off the chair lift. Visualise yourself putting your skis on, now your sticks, goggles or glasses in place and zip up your collar. Visualise all the little details, and then set off down a well known run. Feel the sensations of the movements, the pressures against the soles of your feet, the wind on your face. Watch the terrain and the snow texture as it comes towards you. Slow down and stop when you feel your legs becoming tired through continuous bending and stretching in the moguls.

Shedden's (1982: p.25) description of how a skier might mentally rehearse embodies many of the important things known about the subject — the need for quiet, relaxation and the relevance of both the visualisation of performance and imagination of internal feelings and sensations. Mental rehearsal (sometimes called imagery, covert rehearsal, mental practice, etc.) is not a new subject and is certainly not specific to the sporting world. Salespersons spend time rehearsing encounters with prospective buyers, and military personnel are instructed to spend time visualising potential emergencies so they can react quicker and more safely during actual emergencies. In the world of sport there are many reported cases of top players using mental rehearsal to help them prepare for competition. For example, the skier Jean Claude Killy used to 'run every slalom gate in his mind's eye' just before sleeping the night prior to a competition, and Jack Nicklaus (Nicklaus, 1974: p.49) reports the same kind of 'movie making' in relation to his own golf:

> I never hit a shot, not even in practice, without having a very sharp, in-focus picture of it in my head. It's like a colour movie. First, I 'see' the ball where I want it to finish, nice and white and sitting up high on the bright green grass. Then the scene quickly changes and I 'see' the ball going there: its path, trajectory and shape, even its behaviour on landing. Then there is a sort of fade-out and the next scene shows me making the kind of swing that will turn the previous images into reality.

In athletics, top jumpers spend time during their preparation before the run-up, rehearsing the approach, take-off and flight technique. In fact, top performers in many sports — both team and individual sports — spend time thinking about their performance and testify to the value of mental rehearsal of one kind or another.

Why mentally practice?

Mental rehearsal has a place both as a pre-competition strategy (Cox, 1986) and as an aid to learning. Whilst this book is concerned primarily with the latter there is common ground in both approaches. Traditionally, mental rehearsal has been viewed within the learning context and research has examined the relative benefits of mental practice versus physical practice. The classic experimental paradigm has used three groups of subjects, one of which learns a new skill with physical practice, one group learns using mental practice alone and the third group acts simply acts as a control. The typical finding is that the physical practice group performs best overall, followed by the mental practice group and the control group. It seems that mental rehearsal is not as good as physical practice but is significantly better than no practice at all.

This finding begs a lot of questions. For example, why is mental practice beneficial? How should mental practice be carried out? What should be practised? In relation to the first question, a number of answers have been proffered. It is reckoned by some investigators that mental practice causes the same neural mechanisms to be used as would be employed during physical practice — a neural learning effect (Ulrich, 1967). Others propose that mental practice is accompanied by minute physical movements that resemble the actions themselves (e.g., Suinn, 1979). In this way physical and mental practice provide similar kinds of motor output — feedback experiences. And some investigators conclude that mental practice primarily serves a perceptual function whereby the learner begins to understand more clearly how to avoid distracting stimuli and concentrate attention. Minas (1978) adopts the position that mental practice helps the learner to understand 'how' movements are carried out or sequenced (if they are comprised of overlapping elements) and she provides evidence to support the beneficial effect of mental practice. In a related way, Ryan (1981) suggests that mental practice is an indirect way of mobilising the 'unconscious mind' and thereby provides the learner with a method of solving perceptual problems. He says (p.163):

> There is the suspicion that the unconscious can attack a problem relentlessly and constantly, even though the approach is not in the traditional manner. After the conscious has been working on a problem (a period of mental practice), it may yield an insight to the unconscious, though we don't know by what process. One of the most famous incidents in which the unconscious produced an insight was that of Archimedes proclaiming 'Eureka' in the bathtub.

It could be that this applies to situations where the learner is having particular difficulties in learning a new movement. The author, for example, can remember trying to learn an upstart on the high bar. Despite dozens of attempts and much cajoling he could still not manage to raise his body above the bar. Intense mental practice did not seem to help immediately but, following a week's lay off, the first attempt produced success. Somehow, there was a 'Eureka' effect and everything clicked!

In relation to competition, mental rehearsal is thought to have a number of desirable benefits. Hardy and Fazey (1986) suggest that mental practice can be used to help the performer psychologically warm-up, it being especially valuable at times when there is a time lapse between physical warm up and competition proper, e.g., as in gymnastics or ski-racing. Cox (1986) indicates that in addition to the learning effect of mental rehearsal, it helps the athlete prepare 'body and mind' for activity as well as helping to control/focus his/her attention on factors relevant to the task in hand. Rushall (1979) underlines the importance of mental rehearsal and goes as far as to suggest that mental rehearsal should be an essential part of the individual's preparation for competition. However, he qualifies his comments by saying that it is not a substitute for active practice and is only effective with elite or highly skilled performers. In addition, it is a skill which takes time and has to be learned. Greenbank (1991) suggests mental imagery can be an effective way of reviewing failure at a task and of curing anxieties — especially in high risk sports such as rock climbing.

From what has been said above and from the evidence available, it seems that mental practice can make a contribution to skill acquisition. A number of questions still remain however. What form of mental rehearsal is best? How/where/when should it take place? Let's examine these questions.

Different types of mental rehearsal

In its broadest sense, mental rehearsal constitutes any kind of conscious imagery whether it be of an event, movement, situation or series of actions. It might be a process of re-construction where say a performance which has already been executed is reviewed and 'run again' (either, as it was, or should have been), or it could be a process of construction where a proposed or anticipated performance is 'previewed'. It might be purely visual in nature in which case the learner watches him/herself or another performer undertaking an activity (visual imagery) or it might be kinesthetic in which case the learner goes through a technique and tries to imagine muscular and joint sensations, as well as the timing, forces and positions of the various movements. And of course, it might be a combination of both.

It is thought that visual imagery is better for less-experienced learners because it is much easier to visualise than to recall or construct kinesthetic sensations. The expert is better prepared to use kinesthetic imagery because he/she possesses better defined self-images and is able to recall internal feelings with greater consistency. For the same reason it is easier for beginners to visualise others performing rather than themselves. These are logical conclusions although there is, as yet, no empirical support for this. Cox (1986) pursues this line by suggesting that it is better for learners to model their mental rehearsals on the perform-ance of good technicians, especially those who are personally known to or admired by the learner (Cox, 1986). The logic for this (and again, there is no hard data to prove the point) is that mental images formed by observing good performers are likely to be more accurate than those formed from introspection alone.

Whitmore (1982) discusses a number of variations on the above methods. He talks for example, about 'creative imagination' where the individual attempts to imagine that he/she is actually someone else — perhaps a world class athlete — and even tries to feel what it is like to be that person. Whitmore also refers to 'symbolic imagination' where the individual not only emphasises technique, but also imposes a specific 'quality' on that rehearsal. For example, the expressions, 'ski like a seagull' or 'swim like a dolphin' suggest styles of moving and moods which can be used to direct visualisation in particular ways.

When is mental rehearsal most useful?

Mental rehearsal is best thought of as an adjunct to physical practice. It may be a particularly valuable aid at times during injury, whilst travelling or at other times when not practising.

For learners, it is probably most effective just prior to performance, especially in brief activities such as high jumping or sprint starting. It helps the learner focus attention on the critical elements in a movement or movement sequence and helps him/her prepare by minimising the effects of potentially distracting influences. For example, a child about to try a vault might imagine completing the whole action. He/she could break down the action into three phases — approach, flight on, flight off — observe each action in sequence and note the key element of each phase. Following an attempt at the vault, the learner could engage in mental rehearsal once more as a way of reviewing errors and comparing what is expected with actual performance. The sequence — mental rehearsal, practice, mental rehearsal — is commonly used by learners and seems a very natural thing to do. The importance of mental rehearsal immediately prior to action should be underlined. Under these circumstances, transfer should be greatest, images should be clearest and feedback review most informative.

Mental practice is only beneficial if the skill level of the learner is reasonably consistent. This implies that the learner must have already undergone an extended period of physical practice. As Ryan (1981) indicates, the learner can only profit from mental rehearsal if the input is good. Models must be technically correct or else the learner rehearses techniques that are wrong and just consolidates errors. This applies, of course, not only to models of the learner, but also to those of other people which the learner uses. Cox (1986) makes the point that models for rehearsal should be of someone whose performance has been studied at close hand many times previously. In addition, they must not be too far removed from the learner's own style and performance level. This would seem to make sense from what was said in Chapter 5 about positive transfer.

Mental rehearsal is linked with motivation. It is extremely difficult to do if the learner doesn't believe in its importance. Highly motivated people automatically think a lot about their sport and are more likely to accept mental rehearsal as a viable training aid. For those who are not motivated to improve their skill levels by using mental rehearsal techniques, there is little point in trying.

How to mentally rehearse

Mental rehearsal is a learned skill which takes considerable time and dedication to develop fully. One cannot just decide to 'have a go' and expect immediate results. For one thing, mental practice demands a relaxed state of mind and this itself demands control and practice (see later). Also, the learner needs to know how to do it and also needs to know what material to include. Learning how to rehearse comes about through practice and evaluation. The learner for example, can recite to him/herself or speak to another person. The coach may listen to a tape recording or question the learner about rehearsal strategies. Bull (1991) argues for individualised mental training programmes.

The problem with any kind of conscious mental activity is that the mind is very limited in the amount of information it can handle at any one time. For example, it is very easy to forget a telephone number before dialling is complete. Mental rehearsal therefore, has to be concentrated and only selected items dealt with. This presents problems for those activities such as team games which extend over time and constantly change. Rushall (1979) makes the point that mental rehearsal is still applicable in these circumstances, but the activity must be broken down into smaller segments. Thus a soccer player might rehearse in turn a series of set plays or possible outcomes to an encounter with the defense, whilst a swimmer might rehearse each length of a distance swim. Another strategy would be to visualise a lengthy activity in its entirety first (e.g., a long rock climb or a tumbling routine) and then start again, but focus only on certain parts. The same problem does not exist for repetitive or short-duration activities such as high jumping, or tennis serving. Here, the learner does not have an information overload problem and can probably rehearse the action many times before actual practice.

Most authorities agree that mental rehearsal should mirror as closely as possible the exact circumstances prevailing during practice including for example, use of the same equipment and the same working area. In addition, movements should be rehearsed in their entirety (it would be pointless — and perhaps impossible — to stop a somersault in mid-flight or rehearse a high jump approach without the actual jump) and with the same speed and timing as actual performance. This idea is based on the 'neural model' of mental rehearsal, which proposes that actual performance and mental rehearsal stimulate the same underlying nervous mechanisms. Mental rehearsals should also have a successful outcome. The rehearsal of errors is likely to increase the possibility of errors in performance. It is not easy to think always in such a positive manner, especially for a learner, and it demands a lot of self-discipline, which again underlines the fact that mental rehearsal is a learned skill.

Mental rehearsal is thought to be most effective if it includes attention to the feel of actions as well as the sight of them. Kinesthetic imagery provides a 'richer' experience than just a visual picture. This technique however, is only useful with advanced learners who are more attuned to the feel of their movements.

Finally, mental rehearsal must take place when the individual is in a relaxed state of mind. A person who is anxious or thinking about other matters will not be able to focus his attention correctly. Relaxation is an essential foundation upon which the skills required for mental rehearsal are built. There are many different types of relaxation techniques, each of which works by asking the person to focus on different things, for example his/her breathing pattern or alternate contraction and relaxation of muscles. It is not the object of this book to discuss these methods and they are dealt with very comprehensively elsewhere (e.g., Albinson & Bull, 1988; Cox, 1986), but it might be useful to quote a section of script from Hardy and Fazey (1986: p.17) who describe the technique known as Progressive Muscular Relaxation:

> Sit or lie down in your chosen position. Breathe slowly with your lips apart. Concentrate on the slowing of your breathing pattern. I shall begin counting from one to fifteen. As I count, gradually increase the tension in your muscles. One. Two.

Three: squeeze your muscles slightly harder, tense as many of the muscles in your body as you can. Four. Five. Six: clench your fists. Seven. Eight. Nine. Ten. Tense your thighs. Eleven. Twelve: squeeze harder. Thirteen: and now really hard. Fourteen: and finally as hard as you can. Fifteen: and relax. Focus on your breathing, and relax for a moment. Feel the relaxation spreading and enjoy the sensation of the easing tension. In a moment or two we shall repeat the exercise. etc., etc..

It is clear that methods such as these require both time to learn and time to apply and therefore are not appropriate for the beginner. At best, the beginner should be encouraged to rehearse what he/she is learning during training and especially just before and immediately following practice, and as he/she gains experience and dedication, he/she should be introduced to sophisticated methods of relaxation and mental training which can be employed outside the training environment. At advanced skill levels, there is little doubt that athletes benefit from relaxation and mental rehearsal, but their complex nature should always be born in mind as has been recently highlighted by Miller (1991). Miller puts forward a good case for an integrated approach to mental rehearsal which co-ordinates with the whole competition schedule.

Motivation

Motivation is inextricably bound up with attitudes, feelings, expectations, needs and emotions. Motivation has both long and short-term qualities. Motivation influences a person's decision to take part in sport and determination to persevere and practice over many years, often under trying conditions. In the short term, motivation is a factor responsible for the intensity or vigour with which a person performs, the momentary quality of their performance, as well as the variability in skill level which occurs from one occasion to the next.

Many people would agree that motivation is a major force which attracts people to sport and encourages them to learn and succeed. However, such a crude analysis does little to increase our understanding of the term. The fact is that despite common usage motivation is a much misused concept. One problem is that it defies easy definition. The intention in this section is not to attempt to provide a comprehensive analysis of the subject (see for example, Straub, 1980 or Suinn, 1980 for major reviews), but to present some broad ideas which demonstrate the relevance of motivation during learning.

Reinforcement-motivation

Earlier we explored in detail the topic of feedback and suggested that it can play an informative role as well as a motivational one. A useful examination of feedback or reinforcement motivation is provided by Rushall and Siedentop (1972). They suggest there are four types of reinforcers which the coach can use and 'experiment' with: social, material, performance and internal reinforcers.

Social reinforcers encompass the positive benefits which can be gained from the presence or comments of other people. The coach may signal "very well done" or a friend may congratulate the learner on a particularly successful effort. Comments such as these, or just public display of performance provide attention and demonstrate approval and recognition by other people. Even, how 'good' a coach appears to be to the learner can have a dramatic influence on his/her performance. This point is brought home by Bland (1979: p.28), a swimming coach:

> There are many ideal qualities that the coach should possess; the most important of these are complete reliability and a real determination to succeed. On the whole swimmers are as good as they believe and as good as their coaches can make them believe. Many swimmers change coaches because they believe the coach at the next pool is a better one and it is often this belief alone that makes them swim better, nothing else.

Social reinforcement is a very powerful motivator. Material reinforcers take the form of tangible payoffs such as certificates, labels, badges, and so on. Rewards like these, which characterise most proficiency award schemes, are useful because they provide concrete proof of success and recognition of performance. They also help formulate status within peer groups.

Performance reinforcers such as time taken, number of attempts, accuracy achieved, provide the learner with specific information about performance and serve to give direction to the learner's efforts. As with material reinforcers they also facilitate social approval.

Internal reinforcers include the feelings which the learner experiences during learning and the personal goals realised during the learning process. For example, a youngster who learns to swim unaided may feel fitter/healthier or feel an independence not present before. These in turn help the youngster maintain interest in swimming and may serve to create new goals for the future.

These four categories are not mutually exclusive. Any single event may have a number of consequences: swimming the length of a pool for the first time may produce social approval from friends, stimulate internal satisfaction and also provide a yardstick for improvement.

With regard to reinforcement in learning, there are a number of issues to discuss. External reinforcement and materialistic rewards such as badges, praise, prestige, etc. (the first three reinforcers defined above) tend to be less important than internal goals such as self-esteem, self-expression, personal satisfaction and self-fulfilment. It is thought that the development of intrinsic motivation leads to more satisfying and long lasting results. Although both kinds may operate together with one sometimes more dominant, external forces are usually shorter-lived in their influence than internal ones. One particular exception is with beginners who are often attracted to sport and stimulated to learn new skills because of tangible external rewards such as certificates and medals which bring prestige and satisfaction. In time, however, external reinforcers such as these are overtaken by internal forms of motivation which keep the learner attracted to sport and encourage greater persistence and performance. In fact, learning as a whole is reflected in a change from dependence on extrinsic sources of motivation/information to internally-generated sources. The coach and teacher can contribute to this process by showing learners who show interest and potential how sport can aid self-realisation, individuality and personal satisfaction.

Rushall and Siedentop (1972) make a number of additional points. Firstly, it is not essential for reinforcement always to be positive. Reinforcement in the form of (for example) praise is beneficial, but only up to a point. Constant praise soon ceases to have an effect and learners should recognise that from time to time they will be told that things are wrong. How the coach or teacher handles these occasions needs to be treated with care if some learners are not to be discouraged. Secondly, coaches should determine the most effective way of providing reinforcement. A coach may find his/her personal comments carry more weight than performance scores, or that the presence of a particular learner within a group spurs on the rest by a disproportionate amount. A sensitive coach should attempt to note the different forces involved in group situations (group dynamics) and maximise those which have the best effect. Thirdly, reinforcement should be individual-based. Comments such as "good work, team" or "that's the way to go" are often ineffective. This applies of course especially to beginners who are searching for outward signs of success and approval. The coach also needs to be sensitive to how the learner reacts to feedback. Some who do not perform according to expectations will lose self-confidence and motivation. Others who are 'emotionally tougher' will respond to harsh words from the coach. Finally, Rushall and Siedentop refer to what may be called the 'quality' of reinforcement. Quality embodies a number of aspects. Timing is critical. Reinforcement should be supplied immediately success is observed. Coaches should reward learners whenever good behaviour is seen — they should utilise every 'teaching moment'. Most important, reinforcement should be variable in its type and emphasis. This refers to the richness of the coach's vocabulary, the manner in which the voice is used (change in volume, pitch, emphasis), the extent of non-verbal communication (facial expression, use of gesture, physical contact with the learner) as well as the proximity of the coach to the learner and the extent of group/individual instruction.

Motivation and the individual

Attempts to encourage motivation should acknowledge individual differences between learners — a sensitivity to dissimilarities among learners with regard to personality, values, reaction to incentives, achievement need, etc. allows the coach to treat each learner as needed.

A person's aspiration level — the goals he/she expects to achieve — often determines the level of performance achieved. In part, aspiration level is dictated by previous successes and failures: satisfying experiences lead to an activity being favourably regarded. The coach can ensure the learner maintains high aspirations by reducing the chances of continual failure. This is achieved by making sure the learner is neither over-confident nor under-confident and is realistically aware of his/her capabilities. There are implications here with regard to setting practical and specific goals for the learner as well as making a true appraisal of past performance. It is worth mentioning that people sometimes fear success because it brings responsibility and prestige which they are unsure of being able to handle. The shy person who is very skilful may not realise his/her full potential because he/she cannot cope with the peer recognition that comes with success. Such problems will be detected by the perceptive coach and need to be managed in a thoughtful manner. It should also be mentioned that a common reason for failure is self-perception of low ability — those who say they won't do very well end up not doing well. Level of aspiration can work both for and against the learner!

Level of aspiration represents the individual's expected performance. The need to achieve is related to level of aspiration but is different in so far as it represents a personality trait of the individual and is highly specific. Need-achievement can be a fairly stable personal quality. People have varying degrees of need-achievement. Those who possess a high need to achieve can sometimes be described quite well. They tend to be extremely persistent, work hard and fast, take reasonable risk, enjoy stress, like to take personal responsibility for their actions and need detailed knowledge of the results of their performances. Singer & Hilmer (1980) suggest that qualities such as these can be nurtured by the coach if certain conditions are met. Many have already been discussed elsewhere in this book, but it is worth noting them again.

1. The coach and learner should engage in joint discussion as to the purposes of a particular practice or programme of work.
2. Goals for the learner should be set which are specific, challenging and attainable. The learner should be involved in the goal-setting process.
3. The procedures for attaining goals should be explored between coach and learner. Learners should be involved in deciding how practices might be constructed and how they fit into a larger programme of work.
4. The learner should be encouraged to maintain a personal record of progress.
5. The coach should work to ensure the maintenance of the learner's self-confidence and improvement of self-image. There is a circular relationship between success, self-image and self-confidence. The more the learner achieves the more confident he/she

becomes, leading in turn to a better self-image. As a consequence of improved self-image the learner perseveres and improves his/her level of skill.

6.   The learner's progress should be evaluated on a regular basis.

McClelland (e.g., McClelland, 1965) has examined those factors which may affect need-achievement. He suggests one of the most critical factors is the manner in which people habitually think about themselves and how they perform. It seems to matter how good the learner perceives him/herself to be. If this is true, there are implications for how learners experience success and failure and the extent to which they are involved in their own learning and training (Fuoss & Troppman, 1981).

An important point which stems from the ideas in this section is that of coach/learner interaction. Singer and Hilmer (1980) argue that the development of need-achievement hinges on an interactive process where ideas can be exchanged and understanding improved. They say (p.58):

> ... achievement can be reflected primarily through the inter-active process, and both the coach and athlete need to be involved in such a way as to establish a working relationship towards the accomplishment and realisation of goals. The command or dictatorial process has inherent flaws in it. On the other hand, allowing the participant free rein in the decision-making process is also a frivolous activity. Yet a fruitful relationship between the participant and leader can emerge with careful planning and thoughtfulness.

These points are underlined in the following extracts from a video discussion between a senior trampoline coach and one of his top performers (National Coaching Foundation, 1987).

> [Coach]: She has always been keen on learning skills. She was never satisfied with doing any movement once and leaving it at that point. Always, she wanted to be better. Coupled with that, from the very beginning she had a good kinesthetic awareness — she responded to what she felt and saw so that she could respond to coaching. She enjoyed that relationship in coach-ing. She's a perfectionist. I think that's important. She wanted her technique to be as good as she could do then, and better than anyone else if possible. I've always felt it important that a performer should understand what it was we were trying to achieve. So this is a two-way process. As a coach, I try to put across in language appropriate what I think the technique should be, how I think a movement should look and feel and I try to explain how this is achieved so there's an understanding of the movement from the very beginning of the earliest experiences. So, all the way along the line we've been improving techniques fundamentally, amplifying them, adding to them

and making that a progressive, understandable process, enjoyed by both of us.

[Athlete]: I like to understand what I'm doing. If I don't understand something, I don't trust it. If I don't trust it, I doubt myself and I get scared to even try the move. Whereas with my coach we always talk about why we are doing what we're doing and what the effect will be if you change something. In this way, I'm more prepared for what happens and do not worry about it all going wrong.

These comments show how skill and need-achievement can be developed through close learner/coach relationships, and although this is perhaps most fruitful with skilled performers who normally enjoy close contact with their coaches, the importance of the coach's involvement in shaping the motivations of learners and developing a positive attitude to learning should not be under-estimated. Syer (1986) expands on these ideas and the reader is directed to his text for further information.

Motivation and the situation

It is well known that certain factors outside the individual's control dictate what sports they play and how well they perform. For example, cultural influences create ambitions and encourage interests in particular sports (cricket is popular in Great Britain and India but not North America). Social expectations created by family, friends and peers can also act as forceful motivators. For example, the presence of other people tends to dampen the performance of lowly skilled individuals and raise the performance of the highly skilled. There are implications here for the way in which the coach or teacher organises groups of beginners, in the sense that individuals should not see themselves as focal points 'on trial'. This will be more of a problem with those who cannot handle the stress of being watched by onlookers or who fear loss of recognition from friends. The coach has to balance potential difficulties like this with the benefits to be gained by learners working together in a group. Skill acquisition may be viewed as a social process in which individuals benefit by reinforcing, informing and motivating one another. The teacher or coach can enrich this process by devising relevant practices in which people both compete against and cooperate with one another.

Another potentially important influence on the learner is the situation or learning context. Research has shown that situations can be contrived in which people think they can do better than expected and consequently do perform better, when in fact there is no scientific basis for them doing so. For instance, in the medical world it has been shown that patients suffering from severe and persistent headaches often improve when they are given medication which they believe to be useful when in fact, it contains nothing more than an inert substance such as sugar. In the educational world, the same thing happens under the banner of 'teacher expectations'. Here, pupils can often do better than predicted because the teacher 'expects' them to do well. With regard to coaching, there are implications for the attitude adopted by coaches in relation to what they expect of learners. The coach who sets high standards and creates a positive atmosphere which is safe and success-ful, will 'push' people along to greater effort and skill levels through positive expectation alone. If the coach can make the learner believe he/she has the potential to succeed and surround him/her with an air of expectancy and success, it is likely the learner will rise to the occasion. This is probably one reason why many successful sports clubs as well as individuals achieve consistently well over many years. We are drawn once again to the cliché — "success breeds success".

Motivation and the task

Aspects of the technique being learned or the practices set by the coach/teacher will influence the amount of interest shown by learners and the extent to which they persist. Activities which contain elements of complexity, physical challenge and relevance will sustain people longer. Part practices which are not seen by learners to have a relationship to the game proper will de-motivate quickly. Even those practices which are appropriate and necessary, but not perceived as such by learners, may bore and turn them away from the sport. Learners must be convinced of the need for drills and skill practices at all times.

Performers at high levels of skill who have to devote intense and long periods of time to training can tire quickly from routine training which is repetitive and uninteresting. Practice should be made interesting and as personally rewarding as possible. It should be varied (change of location, use of visiting coaches, changes in responsibilities, etc.) so that new enthusiasms are generated and existing motivation sustained.

Summary

1. Skilled performance as well as skill learning depends on the refinement of technique and is inextricably linked to 'mental' factors such as mental rehearsal, motivation and need-achievement.
2. The Inner Game approach to learning addresses both the physical and mental components in sport.
3. Proponents of the Inner Game advocate that:
   a. traditional teaching methods are too technically oriented;
   b. critical self-analysis by the learner is an obstacle to success;
   c. learners have a potential to learn which is often never revealed;
   d. trust and confidence in the learner must be engendered by both the learner and the coach;
   e. enhancing body awareness is one of the major keys to success-ful learning.

4. Goal setting is an important strategy for learners and coaches. Clear goals increase confidence and provide direction for practice.
5. Long-term goals should be broken down into intermediate and short-term goals.
6. Goals should be specific, individually oriented, challenging, attainable, realistic and measurable.
7. Product goals are appropriate in the long-term whilst process goals are more applicable in the short term.
8. Mental rehearsal can be a valuable aid to learning. There are a number of theories as to why it works, e.g., physiological, perceptual.
9. Mental rehearsal can take a number of forms and take advantage of all the major senses.
10. Mental rehearsal is beneficial for learners who already have substantial experience, but is especially useful for experts. It is a learned skill in its own right.
11. Motivation has both short-term and long-term qualities and is responsible for, among other things, the intensity with which people perform/learn, as well as the extent of their commitment to sport.
12. Reinforcement has four dimensions: social, material, performance and internal reinforcement. They are not mutually exclusive.
13. Good teaching/coaching recognises the individual nature of motivation with regard to, e.g., personality, values, achievement need, reaction to incentives, the situation and the task in hand.

Discussion questions

1. Take a sport in which you coach or teach. Would you say you dwell too much on technical matters at the expense of others such as the learner's goals and motivations.?
2. In your own learning can you remember occasions when you have been too self-critical of your performance? Was this a good or bad thing?
3. What are the disadvantages of self-criticism? List, say, three points.
4. Can you think of any evidence to support Gallway's view that the potential of most learners is never realised?
5. Take a sport familiar to you. What steps would you take to direct the learner's attention to the 'process' of movement instead of the 'product' of movement? In other words, how would you sensitize the learner to internal feedback?
6. Is it necessary to talk to learners about the precise goals for every training session?
7. How easy is it to establish goals for large groups of learners? Does 'ability grouping' help?
8. How would a coach assess whether or not a particular goal was attainable?

9.   What reasons militate against the use of mental rehearsal with beginners?
10. When would a player in a team game (such as hockey) employ mental rehearsal during the game itself?
11. Do you think that 'visual' rehearsal is appropriate for open skills such as team games, whereas 'kinesthetic' rehearsal is more appropriate for closed skills such as gymnastics?
12. How important is the coach's belief in the learner? Do you think people can be pushed to higher levels if they are made to think they have the potential?

References

Albinson, J.G. & Bull, S.J. (1988) *A mental game plan: A training program for all sports*. Eastbourne, UK: Sports Dynamics.

Bland, H. (1979) *Competitive swimming*. East Ardsley: EP Publishing Ltd.

Bull, S.J. (1991) Personal and situational influences on adherence to mental skills training. *Journal of Sport and Exercise Psychology*, **13**, 121–132.

Byrne, T. (1986) Introduction. *Coaching Focus*, **4**, 1.

Cox, R. (1986) *Psychological preparation for competition — Mental rehearsal* (Coach Education Module 8). Edinburgh: The Scottish Sports Council.

Crimble, S. (1982) *Inner sport — A look in*. Scottish Journal of Physical Education, **10**, 1–3.

Fisher, S. (1991) Inner game teaching for the P.E. teacher. *The Bulletin of Physical Education*, **27**, 1, 20–23.

Fuoss, D.E. and Troppman, R.J. (1991) *Effective coaching: A psychological approach*. New York: Wiley & Sons.

Gallway, T. and Kriegal, R. (1977) *Inner skiing*. New York: Random House.

Greenbank, A. (1991) All in the mind. *Climber & Hillwalker*, **XXX**, 12, 40–42.

Hardy, L. (1986) How can we help performers? *Coaching Focus*, **4**, 2–3.

Hardy, L. (1990) Importance of psychological factors in affect on performance. *Coaching Focus*, **15**, 4–5.

Hardy, L. and Fazey, J. (1986) *Mental preparation for competition* (Key course resource pack). Leeds: National Coaching Foundation.

Jones, C. (1974) *Sunday Times*, October 13th.

Matthews, S. (1991) Sports psychology: A consumer perspective. *The Psychologist*, **4**, 4, April.

McClelland, D.C. (1965) Toward a theory of motive acquisition. *American Psychologist*, **20**, 321–333.

Miller, B. (1991) Mental preparation for competition — A system for success. *Coaching Focus*, **18**, 3–5, 1991.

Minas, S. (1978) Mental practice of a complex perceptual-motor skill. *Journal of Human Movement Studies*, **4**, 102–107.

Mutrie, N. (1985) *Goal setting*. Coach Education Modules. Edinburgh: Scottish Sports Council.

National Coaching Foundation (1987) *Improving Techniques*. Level 1 video. Leeds: National Coaching Foundation, 1987.

Nicklaus, J. (1974) *Golf my way*. London: Simon & Schuster.

Rintala, J. (1991) The mind-body revisited. *QUEST*, **43**, 260–279.

Rushall, B.S. (1979) *Psyching in sport*. London: Pelham Books Ltd., 1979.

Rushall, B.S. & Siedentop, D. (1972) *The development and control of behaviour in sports and physical education*. Philadelphia: Lea & Febiger.

Ryan, F. (1981) *Sports and psychology*. Englewood Cliffs, N.J.: Prentice Hall Inc.

Schubert, F. (1985) *Psychology from start to finish*. Toronto: Sports Books Publisher.

Shedden, J. (1982) *Skilful skiing*. East Ardsley, West Yorks.: EP Publishing Ltd.

Singer, R.N. & Hilmer, R. (1980) Achievement training. In Suinn, R. (Ed.), *Psychology in sports: Methods and applications*. Minneapolis: Burgess Publishing Co.

Straub, W.F. (Ed.) (1980) *Sport psychology: An analysis of athlete behaviour*. Ithaca, N.Y.: Mouvement Publications.

Suinn, R. (Ed.) (1980) *Psychology in sports: Methods and applications*. Minneapolis: Burgess Publishing Co.

Syer, J. (1986) *Team spirit: The elusive experience*. London: Kingswood Press.

Ulrich, E. (1967) Some experiments on the function of mental training in the acquisition of motor skills. *Ergonomics*, **10**, 411–419.

Whitmore, J. (1982) The use of imagery in sports education. Scottish Journal of Physical Education, **10**, 1–7.

140

Chapter 8

EVALUATION OF SKILL

Importance of evaluation

In the first chapter the multi-role nature of coaching was examined. One of the roles described the coach as a scientist or analyst. Analysis is central to much of the coach's or teacher's work and pervades most things including for example the examination of injuries, the assessment of motivation, the appraisal of 'opposition' and the evaluation of performance. Obviously, anyone who is concerned with helping others to improve their skill or knowledge should analyse whether improvement and gains have taken place. However, the literature on skill evaluation *per se* is very scarce. One probable explanation for this lies in the view that skill is apparently very easy to assess. In many ways this is true. It would appear simple to note how well a person performs at the start of practice (e.g., an athlete can jump 1.65m) and observe their level of attainment sometime later (he/she can now jump 1.85m). One just has to look in order to see! To adopt this stance, however, is to deny the complexity of human learning and also underplay the value of the many methods available for analysis. It also assumes that analysis applies only to the learner. What about the coach? Should the coach's efforts also be monitored and if so by whom? And what about the likes of equipment, clothing and training methods? Should these also come under scrutiny? The answer should be yes to all these.

Evaluation is a complex subject. Rowntree (1979) has identified five dimensions which can be applied with varying emphases to the evaluation of skill. Let us examine each in turn.

Elements of evaluation

Why evaluate?

Why is there a need to evaluate? What are the outcomes of the evaluation process? There are a number of reasons.

1. To give the learner feedback which is accurate and meaningful, the coach must examine the learner's behaviour and compare performance with either his/her own model of 'correctness' (some kind of reference of excellence held in the coach's memory) or the learner's previous performance. Observation, error diagnosis and rectification are all critical ingredients within this process.

2. To determine if goals established during a practical session or over a training season have been met. For example, is a new, voluntary trampolining routine ready to be used in competition?

3. To determine if a particular method of teaching is appropriate (e.g., a procedure for introducing a novel and complicated gymnastic stunt).

4. To record a learner's progress over a period of time. For example, a coach may examine a high jumper's training diary to assess changes in height jumped over a season.

5. To provide a record of achievement for the purposes of certification, motivation or selection. For beginners to a new sport one of the attractions is the attainment of a proficiency award. Awards such as those designed by governing bodies of sport or those designed by the coach or teacher to suit local needs provide tangible recognition of achievement and also help sustain interest and motivation. For experts, the coach may evaluate for the purposes of selection (e.g., team selection, international honours).

6. To provide a means of assessing excellence in competition (e.g., an ice skating championship or swimming gala).

7. To give some insight into the performance potential of people, as when a talent scout surveys an opponent's players, i.e., scouting.

8. Another, less obvious reason for evaluation is to provide 'models' of what should be expected in games. For example, in basketball, it is likely that a player or team will not score every attempt at a basket. The coach may wish to determine an acceptable level of error in order to provide a basis for evaluating team performance on subsequent occasions. 'Modelling' involves the systematic collection of information over many games. We shall return to this later under the heading of match analysis.

What is evaluated?

Secondly, what should be evaluated? What elements should be examined by the coach or teacher? Here, there are a number of skill components which may be relevant such as technique (as in ski jumping), timing (as in striking a ball), accuracy (as in archery), distance gained (as in javelin throwing) and frequency (as in soccer — number of goals). The emphasis will depend on the sport in question as well as the particular learner's problem. For example, a long jumper may not be achieving his/her best because of a faulty technique position on take-off. The coach may concentrate attention on the last few strides to see how the error develops. Knowing what to evaluate involves informed judgement based on experience. In the example, it is no good telling the long jumper to "try harder to hit the board at a better angle". The coach has to identify the underlying fault.

How does the coach evaluate?

Thirdly, how should the coach assess? Which technique amongst all those available is the most valid and appropriate? Recent research

(Sharp, 1988) shows that coaches rely mostly on their own personal judgements or those of other people to make decisions about a person's skill. This may be appropriate in many circumstances but there may be problems. The most important is the validity of what the coach sees. Lee, Lishman & Thomson (1982) have shown through a film analysis of the approach run in long jumping that there is a difference between what the coach notices and what the athlete actually does. Specifically, they demonstrated that athletes modified their approach near the take-off board whereas the coach thought they 'programmed' the entire run from the start. Problems such as this can be avoided through the use of objective methods (e.g., notation, computer analysis, practical tests) but, despite the importance coaches attach to these and other 'objective' type approaches, their own observations are often rated much more highly (Sharp, 1988).

How should data be interpreted?

Fourthly, how should coaches interpret the data they collect about their learners? The coach needs to explain and make sense from such data. This is a fairly obvious stage and probably happens automatically. Observations may give the coach pleasure because he/she sees rapid improvement or they may cause him/her to reflect on a problem whose solution is unclear. They may produce disappointment and suggest his/her approach is not right. The coach's assessment of the learner will invariably have both emotional and informative connotations.

How should coaches respond to evaluation?

Lastly, the coach or teacher must decide how to respond. Usually, the coach will respond by telling the learner about technical problems and how they can be tackled. Remedial work, further practice or different tasks will be set as a way of rectifying errors, motivating learners and solving difficulties.

If the coach is to be effective then all of these issues listed above must be addressed. Some will dominate, and their importance will depend on the sport in question (e.g., methods of analysis for outdoor sports may be quite different to those for indoor sports) as well as the coach's knowledge. In respect of the latter point, we now turn to some technical issues.

Definitions

A number of expressions have been used, e.g., measurement, evaluation, assessment, analysis which, although used interchangeably, have distinct meanings. A measurement is the actual score or value which a person may be given (e.g., an athlete runs a mile in 6 mins 30 secs.). Measurements may be objective and hence agreed by everyone (15 successful free shots from 20) or subjective in nature ("she has a very clumsy free throwing technique"). Often, objective measurements are more easily obtained from the outcome of skilled actions (e.g., height

jumped, number of goals scored, time taken) as opposed to the performance or movements themselves (e.g., figure skating performance, ski-
jumping style). Technique *per se* is more frequently examined in a
subjective manner (although not always — see later in this Chapter) and
is one reason for disagreement about how good people are (e.g., consider
the varying marks awarded to competitors in Olympic gymnastics or ice
skating competitions). This underlines a key problem of evaluation which
is that the assessment of an individual's skill often reflects the skill of the
observer (usually the coach or teacher) and not just that of the individual
him/herself! Assessment is the word given to the actual process of taking
measurements. The procedure adopted which makes up the assessment
is called a test (e.g., Leger 20m shuttle run, Johnson basketball test). A
test normally includes the protocol, instructions to subjects, equipment
required, methods of scoring, etc.. The word evaluation is a more
encompassing one and includes not only the process of assessment but
also that of judgement which involves some kind of decision making
based on the raw measurements. Coaches and teachers may not always
measure learners for the purpose of evaluation, at least not initially. For
example, an athlete may keep a training diary recording such things as
daily resting pulse, weekly weight, number of hours trained, etc., but the
coach may not examine it until some time has passed. At the end of this
period, the coach may use the data to identify weaknesses or strengths.
Only then is the coach evaluating the athlete.

A distinction can be made between formative and summative
evaluation. Formative evaluation takes place all the time as the coach
monitors players, makes changes, provides feedback and generally deals
with moment to moment learning problems as they arise. Formative
evaluation is concerned with the provision of information, the diagnosis
of errors, the improvement of skill as well as the improvement of the
coach's instructional techniques. In contrast, summative evaluation is
concerned with the final or overall evaluation of an individual and is often
used for selection or classificatory purposes. The evaluation of a season's
conditioning programme, the use of a competition to select an Olympic
squad or the testing of a new proficiency award scheme following lengthy
field monitoring are examples of summative evaluation. Summative
evaluation provides a more reliable index of a learner's skill level, but it
often lacks detail because it summarises many performances. Reliability
is one of several important criteria which should prevail when the coach
approaches the topic of measurement. Let us now look at these criteria.

Measurement concepts

Later in the chapter we will address the various ways in which skill can
be monitored. Before we do this it is important to consider the criteria
which these techniques must follow in order for them to be meaningful
and useful. Measurements can easily lose their credibility if certain
criteria are not met. Consider for example, the measurement of a person's

sprinting ability using a hand-held stopwatch. This technique lends itself to all kinds of errors depending on the skill of the person using the watch, how it is used and the quality of the actual device itself. The usefulness of any data depends on at least four characteristics: validity, reliability, objectivity and sensitivity.

Validity

Validity refers to the extent to which a testing procedure measures what it sets out to measure. If a coach wishes to examine the sprinting technique of his/her athletes, the method chosen must actually measure sprinting technique. If it measures something in addition, e.g., the athlete's motivation or level of fitness then it is not wholly valid. Validity is the most important of all criteria and is often the most difficult one to achieve, especially with regard to skill evaluation. If a coach is measuring say fitness, the problem of validity is easier to resolve because the techniques for measuring fitness are well-established and better defined.

The assessment of validity hinges on the methods available to test or measure the parameter in question. It transpires that whilst fitness is relatively simple to measure (e.g., local arm endurance — number of pull ups) skill is not. How, for example, do you assess a person's ability in volleyball? It may be easy to monitor individual elements such as service reception or spiking consistency which are simple to isolate, but the ability to employ these techniques in the game situation, teamwork, tactical awareness, determination, etc., are more complicated qualities which do not always lend themselves to objective measurement.

In order to examine validity the technique chosen to measure the skill or technique in question must be shown to bear a close similarity to some other standard method which is valid (sometimes called a criterion). For example, a coach who selects players for a national badminton squad may decide to use as a guideline the observations and subjective impression of other senior coaches. Whether or not this is a valid method will only be revealed in retrospect. If it transpires that most of the players chosen succeed at international level, then it can be assumed that the method is valid. Otherwise, the method is not. Such a technique of assessing players is known as a qualitative method. A quantitative method would yield objective data about a person, e.g., number of free shots scored out of 20. Such a test would be a highly valid test of free shooting ability, but it may not be a valid test of basketball playing ability. In order to assess skill in a game such as basketball it would be necessary to devise a whole battery of tests, each of which measures the essential elements of the game, including not only specific techniques but also the many ways in which the players combine and work as a team. We shall return to this idea later.

A full discussion of validity is beyond the scope of this book. There are several kinds of validity of which two should be mentioned briefly. Concurrent validity is the one just mentioned and refers to tests which assess present skill level for the purpose of providing current information (e.g., how good is the back stroke technique of a swimmer). Tests which have predictive validity attempt to identify skill at some future point in time. Scouting is a good example. Tests which attempt to look into the future run obvious risks because many things happen to people in between the time of measurement and the time when they subsequently perform, and these things can influence the manner in which they learn or perform.

Validity is always a matter of degree; tests are neither completely valid nor completely invalid. The assessment of skill is always a function of many factors. The environmental conditions under which the assessment takes place (e.g., the scout watching a potential player in appalling weather conditions) as well as the characteristics of those being assessed (e.g., age, gender, skill level) influence the accuracy and hence validity of assessment.

Reliability

There is often a need to measure skill on two different occasions, e.g., to determine the extent of learning. In these cases the method adopted must measure the same thing, i.e., it must be reliable or dependable. If a test (which may be simple visual observation) lacks reliability or consistency in what it measures then there is no basis for comparison, and hence in a learning context, no basis for providing learners with useful feedback. To give an example, suppose a coach wished to measure a gymnast's control in performing back flips. The coach might measure the number of sequential back flips that could be completed by laying out a length of gymnastic matting and asking the gymnast to complete as many as possible. This would be a reliable test if the coach ensured that the same conditions prevailed (e.g., same time of day, same mat, same gymnasium, same instructions, no injuries etc.) and that the gymnast was allowed a reasonable number of attempts on both occasions. Repetition is critical to both validity and reliability. The assessment must yield a 'representative' picture of a person's performance in the same way that opinion polls gather data from many people. In professional soccer, some teams for example, take potential newcomers to the home ground for a week and watch them train and perform in every possible situation. This is done to maximise the coach's ability to predict correctly good talent. Repeated 'viewing' such as this is not always possible, as seen in Olympic competition when athletes usually only have one or two attempts to demonstrate skill.

The basis for reliability is the manner in which a test is administered. If the test is an objective one (how many baskets scored from 100 free throws) then it should not be difficult to ensure that everything (facilities, equipment, layout, instructions, clothing, scoring, etc.) remains constant. With subjective-type assessments such as the scouting example mentioned before, reliability is more difficult to establish but is aided through the use of a set of guidelines or performance criteria. Judges in gymnastic or trampolining competitions for example work to a preset list of criteria (approach run, technique in flight, control on landing, etc.) so that every athlete is given the same test. Without rigid checklists it is impossible for the judge or coach to be unbiased when observing.

It is relatively easy to establish reliability providing the methods of measuring skill are not too complex or subjective. Also, in a test/re-test situation where differences from one performance to another are under scrutiny, what happens to people in between (history) must also be considered. A test may be highly reliable but may not appear so because the learner has experienced something between the two test occasions which has affected performance (e.g., an injury, extra coaching). Finally, it should be noted that a test may be reliable but not valid (e.g., the use of an accurate stopwatch to measure hurdling technique may give a very accurate recording of speed, but it will not record details about technique). Also, a test which is valid is, by default also reliable.

Objectivity

Objectivity is a form of reliability in which one possible source of error — that of differences in test administrators — is examined. The best way to explain this term is to give an example. Assume that two different coaches each examine, say, a basketball player, with a view to deciding whether he/she should be included in the first team. Further, assume that all factors which could cause a difference to exist between the two observations are controlled (e.g., the player is watched during the same game for the same length of time and each coach views from the same position). If these assumptions are correct, the only reason for differences to exist between the two observations is the fact that two different people are measuring the player. If there are differences, the test or observation lacks objectivity. Objectivity is important in cases where assessments have to be made by different people. This occurs frequently in skill, especially competitive gymnastics and ice skating. Here, the marks awarded by the various judges often differ (political bias, judging experience?) and the mere fact that they do differ reveals a lack of objectivity. The same happens with proficiency awards which are employed by many sporting bodies. By definition, proficiency schemes are administered by different people and are the responsibility of many coaches. It follows therefore that different standards and criteria may be applied.

Lack of objectivity may not be a critical problem at beginner level where simple badges or certificates are at stake, but higher up the performance ladder where the focus is on prestigious medals or team selection, it is vital that objectivity be as tight as possible. Of course, when the same coach assesses from one occasion to the next, which would be the normal coach/learner relationship, then bias and objectivity are not a problem.

Finally, the way to increase objectivity is to ensure that all those people who evaluate players or learners are mindful of the same performance criteria and procedures for carrying out the test. Most proficiency award schemes, for example, provide the user with clear instructions, diagrams and guidelines. However, when evaluation is more subjective it is easier for bias, related for example, to the coach's experience, or nationalism to enter.

Sensitivity

Sensitivity refers to the extent to which a test can distinguish between two similar performances. For example, a stopwatch which registers only tenths of a second would not be a very sensitive tool for assessing the performance of top level sprinters — they might all achieve the same score even though positioned quite differently. An electronic system which records to hundredths of a second would be more sensitive (and of course more valid than a hand-held stopwatch). A coach who just remarks "good" or "bad" is not being very sensitive and such comments provide little information on occasions when more detail is required.

It is easy to devise objective systems to differentiate performances (the film system used for photo-finishes in athletics is a good example), but for the coach making a subjective appraisal it is more difficult. The ability to detect the difference between two athletes (e.g. completing the same diving routine) or two performances from the same person is fraught with problems. The detection of fine differences hinges on a detailed knowledge of technique — what does perfect performance look like, what kinds of errors can occur, how do common faults arise — as well as close attention to specific elements of the technique. The coach cannot simply adopt an overall perspective and hope to isolate particular aspects: attention must be selective and consistent.

There is also the problem of time lapse between successive performances. During even a brief time lapse the coach risks forgetting details from the first observation or distorting it in some way. These kinds of problems are helped with the use of video film which provides the coach (and judge) with replay and slow-motion facilities which allow fine discriminations to be made. In addition, video strengthens all the criteria — validity, objectivity and reliability. Video will be looked at later in the chapter and interested readers are directed to the excellent text by Lyons devoted entirely to the subject (Lyons, 1987).

Let us now turn our attention to the methods used by coaches and teachers to monitor and evaluate skill.

How is skill measured?

The evaluation of skill is complicated for a number of reasons. Sports differ in many ways; some require team work whilst others involve just individual performance; skill in some rests on the outcome of performance whilst with others performance itself is the focal point. In addition, a number of different analytical approaches can be adopted (subjective/ objective, quantitative/qualitative). The method also depends on the aims of the person making the assessment (e.g., to fault find, to select for a team, to motivate) as well as the resources available to that person. One of the reasons why Sharp (1988) for example, found many coaches favour a subjective approach is that they do not have access to more sophisticated methods nor do they have the time to employ them. We shall return to these matters later, but for the present a useful start can be made by looking at the methods depicted in Figure 20 .

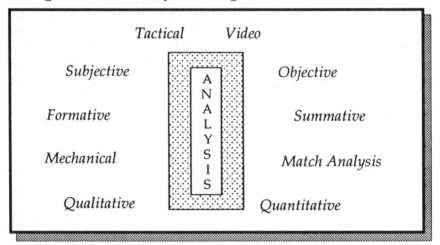

Figure 20:   Some of ways in which performance can be examined. These methods are not mutually exclusive.

Watkins (1987a, 1987b) presents a useful way of categorising these methods. He distinguishes between team games/sports and individual sports. Broadly, match/player analysis and sports skill tests apply to team sports such as volleyball and soccer, whilst movement analysis (quantitative and qualitative) applies to individual sports such as athletics and swimming. There is an overlap with the latter also being used to examine movement in team sports. Firstly, let us consider individual sports and in particular the methods used to describe and analyse the technique and mechanical efficiency of the performer's movements. Watkins suggests there are two categories of movement analysis; qualitative and quantitative.

Qualitative analysis

Qualitative analysis is based on direct visual observation of the learner and results in a more-or-less subjective evaluation of the movement under consideration. It is used in teaching and coaching to provide the learner with feedback and also in the context of judging for the purpose of differentiating between individuals. It is a two-stage process involving the observation and identification of any discrepancies between expected and actual performance and diagnosis of the cause of any discrepancies. The ability to observe and know what to look for is critical. If the coach's observations are poor then very general or incorrect instruction will follow. The coach's ability to do this rests on his/her personal experience of performing as well as coaching experience, but also a knowledge of what good technique looks like and the mechanical principles which underpin good technique.

There are many ways in which movement can be observed systematically but in all cases it essential for the observer to establish clear criteria (e.g., noting the distance between the basketball dribbler's body and the ball or the position of the hands in relation to the body in swimming). Radford (1991) argues that the more accurate the teacher's observations then the better he/she is able to provide specific feedback and assessments. Brown (1982) describes several observation strategies, of which the sequential approach is one. Here, the coach formulates a mental checklist of the body configurations at different stages of the movement such as that shown in Figure 21, and compares the learner's actions with such a model.

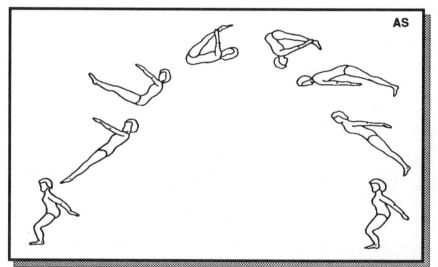

Figure 21: Systematic visual observation where the coach views performance in terms of well-defined sequential stages.

This is a very common method but has certain limitations. It may be based on the technique of elite performers when in fact such a model may not apply to all learners. In addition, whilst it provides a good basis for the identification of errors, it does not provide a systematic basis for diagnosing the cause of movement errors. In a sense, it only provides a description of what went wrong and not an explanation of why it went wrong. For example, it may be clear that a trampolinist's somersault does not result in a successful landing, but the reason for this may not be immediately apparent. There may be a number of underlying causes which are reflected in the same error. In terms of giving the learner feedback, the focus should not be on the 'symptom' of the problem but the cause. Vanderbeck (1979) has explored this matter with regard to swimming and concludes that not only do beginner swimmers tend to display the same kinds of typical errors once they have mastered the gross movement patterns (which therefore allows the coach/teacher to be selective in observing), but they also reveal common error patterns (see Table 3).

Table 3:   **Errors in the front crawl tend to reveal common patterns where particular problems can often be traced back to particular causes.**

Some Common Errors in the Front Crawl

A. *Head carried too high or lifted too high to breathe.* WHY?
  1. Chest and shoulders too high and facing forward in water (Cause — elevation of upper arm and elbow limited during recovery)
  2. Weight of head causes head, shoulders and upper body to sink (Cause — hands pushing downwards to support sinking body) (Cause — length of pull shortened at rear in order to return to downward push)
  3. Hips and legs too low in water
 	
 B. *Body fails to pull alternately to right and left during arm stroke (failure may occur on both sides or only on non—breathing side)* WHY?
  1. Elevation of upper arm and elbow limited during recovery (Cause — failure to lift elbow for recovery) (Cause — failure to lift elbow above hand) (Cause — failure to keep elbow above hand) (Cause — holding elbow straight during recovery)

This, and some of the preceding points are highlighted in the following extract (NCF, 1987):

> Looking at the world around us is a continuous everyday process and it is all too easy to underrate the importance of a coach developing the skill of systematic observation. To do this you must first of all become familiar with the techniques involved in your sport and the way in which they are applied. Then it is necessary to break down complex movements into simpler elements. You should be aware of how these elements relate to each other — a process of cause and effect. Also, you should know what are the most common faults which beset athletes. As a result of this preparation you will be able to observe an athlete's performance in terms of the relative

success at performing each of the elements. You are rating the effectiveness of each element, giving it so much out of 10 as it were. The idea behind this is to separate the acceptable parts of the athlete's performance from those that need improvement. In fact, you should go further than this and find the element which is weakest of all. You will then have identified the root of the athlete's problem and attention should be focused on this.

The question is, how do you do this? A knowledge of the mechanical principles involved can help here. The mechanical approach involves a deeper level of analysis than the sequential approach described previously and involves a thorough knowledge of the principals which govern linear and angular movement. Using this approach, the coach would view the performance depicted in the diagram above in terms of the actions necessary to produce both height and backward rotation. Lack of height could be explained by poor strength of the leg extensor muscles, inadequate flexing of the hips, knees or ankles, or weak arm thrust. All these relate back to well founded mechanical principles which must be followed for success. This kind of information coupled with a knowledge of the learner provides a very sound basis for evaluating performance and helping learners improve technique.

Qualitative approaches to skill evaluation are practical because they demand little use of sophisticated equipment and other resources. The other category of movement analysis, which Watkins identifies — quantitative analysis — is much more scientific.

Quantitative analysis

Quantitative analysis is based on direct measurements of different aspects of performance. The type of measurements taken depends on the purpose of the analysis. If it is the end result or outcome of a movement or sequence of movements then direct measures can be taken. These include time (e.g., as in running or swimming), distance (as in shot putting or long jumping) and number of points scored (e.g., darts, archery). We shall return to these methods shortly. If however, it is the movement pattern itself or sequence of movements which is important, then measurements are taken indirectly through the use of film or audio recordings and other sophisticated technology.

Movement sequences (which can be defined as a series of bodily postures occurring in sequence) are common in most sports, e.g., a gymnastic routine or the movement of a basketball player on court. A quantitative analysis might monitor the type, duration and/or frequency of discrete movements in the sequence and there are many instances when this is desirable. For example, in soccer, a knowledge of the types of movements exhibited by players (e.g., jogging, sprinting, running) and the duration and/or frequency of these movements will help the coach structure specific physical conditioning programmes for different playing positions. Such information would be obtained from film or video recordings of individual players over several games. In the same way, taking a game such as squash, knowledge of the type of strokes and the success rate of the strokes exhibited by an individual player will help the coach plan future technical sessions. These and other types of match analyses will be discussed later in the chapter.

A movement pattern is the way in which the body as a whole moves in relation to its environment or the way in which the body parts move in relation to one another. Adherence to specific movement patterns tends to be more critical in 'closed' situations, e.g., trampolining, diving, gymnastics, and so the quantitative analysis of movement pattern or technique is more common in these sports. There are two basic types of analysis. With a kinematic analysis the coach is concerned with how the body and/or its segments change their position over time. He/she might examine components such as distance moved, speed and acceleration. To do this requires some kind of permanent recording of the performer, either on video or preferably on high-speed cine film. This is then replayed frame by frame and projected onto a large screen and important details such as body positions recorded. Computerised versions using a 'digitiser' make the task of translating information onto paper much easier. Some examples might help to illustrate the value of this approach. In one study the speed-time curve of a novice sprinter, when compared with that of an international athlete, showed that whilst the novice's start was good, he was weak on maximum speed and the ability to maintain speed (see Figure 22). Such information might help the coach plan suitable conditioning work to strengthen the weak areas.

Figure 22:

    Speed/time curves of two sprinters. The elite athlete is slower than the other in the initial part of the sprint, but then overtakes him and his speed decreases less over the latter part. From Watkins (1988a).

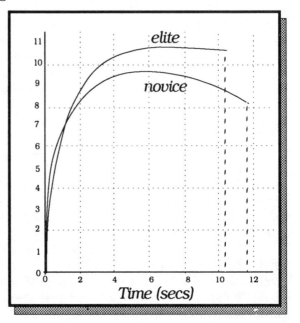

In another study (Stewart and Atha, 1988), a 'CODA 3' scanner was used to monitor the joint positions of archers before the arrow was released (this device is able to record positional accuracy in 3 dimensions, within half a millimetre). The study revealed variations in technique which could not be perceived by the coach's eye or detected by a standard video camera. The data was used to good effect to reduce the archers' errors and improve performance consistency.

In other studies, it has been shown from film analysis that swimmers tire during a race almost wholly because of a reduced stroke length. And, a longitudinal study from 1976 to 1984 found that regardless of swimming stroke and race distance, improvement in swimming speed is due mainly to increases in stroke length. This information has obvious implications for physical conditioning but also for the manner in which coaches work on technique production under stress.

The other type of movement pattern analysis is a kinetic analysis. Kinetic analysis is concerned with the objective measurement of forces acting on the body or between body parts. Film and other techniques are employed to estimate values for force and energy. In one study, the forces exerted by a novice sprinter against the starting blocks were described. A graph depicting the amount of force over time showed that whilst one leg exerted a reasonable amount of force, the other was very weak and lacked power. This difference was not evident from a visual observation of the athlete and thus allowed the coach to rectify a problem in technique which may have gone undetected. In another study, Schleihauf (1979) revealed an important difference in the stroke technique adopted by top swimmers and the technique which coaches believed were adopted by the swimmers. Schleihauf filmed world class swimmers underwater and examined the patterns of movement as well as the lift and drag forces exerted by the hand throughout the stroke cycle. His analysis revealed that the critical factor propelling the body forward is not the action of pulling the hand backward but rather a sculling motion of the hand! In addition, he showed that skilled swimmers display very different movement patterns — the only similarity being the sculling action. This, he suggested, shows that skill in swimming is not so much the ability to learn a strict set of movement patterns, but rather the requirement to develop a stroke pattern which maximises the swimmer's morphology (size, shape, proportions, etc.).

Evaluation methods such as these have not been fully developed in the practical coaching situation and are very much the domain of the laboratory sports scientist and the top athlete/coach who has access to such facilities.

Many other sophisticated techniques exist for examining the fine detail of a person's performance (e.g., electromyography and electrogoniometry) but a discussion of these is beyond the scope of this book. The interested reader is directed to Cooper, Adrian and Glassow (1982) and Watkins (1983).

Watkins's (1987) classification focuses on the evaluation of performance or movement *per se* rather than the outcome of performance. In addition, it looks mainly at individual sports such as swimming and athletics where technique is more important to success. It remains to examine those methods appropriate to team sports and others where the outcome of performance tends to be the barometer of success.

Match analysis

In recent years, a growing interest and body of literature has focused on the subject of match analysis. The media especially have taken advantage of computerised technology to present viewers with match facts and statistics on screen whilst the action of a player or team is in progress. This is found in sports such as volleyball, basketball, American football and so on. Match facts may be relatively comprehensive (as in volleyball where the viewer is given information on serving, control of service, blocking, and smash/dump success rates, etc.,) or quite simple (as in downhill skiing where the computer provides split and final times plus an update of race position). The gathering and accumulation of such information, whether it relates to an individual player or a whole team is known as match analysis. For the coach, match analyses invariably use simple techniques and low technology (often just paper and pencil), together with some kind of notational system for observing action in a structured way. Brackenridge & Alderson (1985) list a number of reasons for this kind of analysis.

Functions of match analysis

- *Modelling*   Modelling is the drawing-up of a complete picture of a particular sport. In the same sense that an electrician uses a detailed and accurate wiring diagram in order to isolate faults in a system, the coach can use a model of the sport as an aid to understanding what is acceptable and expected under certain circumstances. For example, errors are inevitable, but what level of error is acceptable in say penalty kicking in soccer or slip-field catching in cricket? Similarly, the coach may wish to identify the extent to which the team, or a player, demonstrates stereotyped behaviour (e.g., a mid-field soccer player may tend to carry the ball forwards before passing it out to the right wing). Habits such as these may be good or bad depending on whether the opposition or the team can take advantage. Through the compilation of data over a number of games, match analysis can reveal such 'habits' and so provide the coach with a baseline for comparing individual performances.
- *Post mortems*   The most common use is to provide feedback for players or a team, either as a stimulus to alter strategy or as feedback to improve techniques and tactics. As a tool to aid tactical awareness, match analysis is especially useful because it provides a means of objectively recording sequences of actions over a number of games. In a sense, it translates plans which reside in the performer's head and

which are momentary in existence, into concrete recordings for subsequent appraisal.

- *Selection* Player selection is frequently a controversial matter, especially in team sports which involve high levels of judgement and decision making. Match analysis helps supplement the coach's intuition by providing an objective framework for deciding who plays and who does not. An example is seen in athletics where perfor-mance is easily and objectively assessed, which provides selectors with clear data for team or international selection. In a team game, the coach may monitor elements such as number of ball possessions, successful passes, goals scored, and so on.

- *Scouting* Given that the coach has plenty of time for talent spotting, match analysis becomes an excellent back-up tool for supplementing subjective opinion about new players.

The essence of match analysis is quantification. The coach or observer still uses visual observation as a basis for data collection, but in contrast to a qualitative analysis, a permanent record is kept of specific movements or movement outcomes. Typically, a record is kept of the frequency of certain events (e.g., number of winning strokes played from the back court) which is held in some permanent form (e.g., handwritten recording). In addition, the coach or match analyst is guided in his/her observations by a list of specific game elements (e.g., forehand or backhand strokes; strokes only in the frontcourt). The need to permanently store data is crucial and reflects, quite simply, the individual's inability to observe, store and recall vast amounts of information without losing it or biasing it in any way. Research has shown that even trained observers can miss important details, and in addition, experienced teachers and coaches are not necessarily any better in recalling match information than casual observers (Franks & Goodman, 1986). Hence the value of objective and permanent methods of recording information.

Methods of match analysis

The essence of all methods lies in the coach or teacher knowing what questions to ask and therefore what data to collect. He/she then has to choose/devise a system to collect the data. If, for example, a badminton coach wished to know something about the relative success of the various ways a player moved on court (with a view to perhaps introducing different types of movement patterns or changing the emphasis on existing ones) then he/she would need to ask a number of questions, e.g., —

- How many movements are possible?
- What is the nature of each one?
- Where on court do they occur?
- How is the success of a movement pattern examined? etc., etc..

The answers to such questions would clarify the various categories of information to be taken from the game and a system would then have to be devised to collect and store the data. The most frequent technique is to employ a pencil and paper record (see example in Table 4).

Table 4: **Paper and pencil notation system used in badminton to record the movement patterns of a player, the location on court where they take place and whether or not they result in the continuation of a rally.**

Movement Type	Court Location		
	REAR	CENTRE	FRONT
Chassis Lunge	✓✓✓ X✓✓X	✓✓ ✓✓ ✓✓	✓✓✓ X✓
Step Lunge		✓✓ XX	
Chassis		XX✓ X X	X✓ X X
Pivot Run			✓
Pivot Extend			✓✓✓
Hartona Skip	✓✓✓✓ X✓		
Steps			
Run	-		
Run back	X X X	X✓ XXX✓	✓✓ X
Chassis Run	✓	✓✓✓	✓✓

✓ *successful return*   X *unsuccessful return*

Such methods have been used by generations of coaches, bench players and spectators alike. The method involves recording a series of tallies on a prepared sheet such as the one presented above. Totals can be calculated and compared with previous figures either statistically or graphically to give the coach the information required. Methods such as these take time and practice to use skilfully, especially if the game under scrutiny takes place quickly, and they are not entirely immune to error. Also, they do not provide the coach with an immediate analysis. Depending on the complexity of the analysis and length of the game, the analysis may take many hours. Some of these problems are partly solved with the use of video recordings which can be played back slowly and repeatedly (see later) and also computers which can be employed as a direct means of data entry plus analysis tool. A number of current computerised methods employ what is known as a 'concept keyboard' (see Figure 23) which allows simple data entry through the touching of the relevant area on the board. Data analysis which might takes hours manually can be completed in seconds by the computer. In addition, the computer can be used to build up vast quantities of data to establish the kinds of models described earlier. A recent development avoids the use of any kind of keyboard and utilises a voice analyser to recognise commands from the coach which are inputted directly to the computer.

Another method used increasingly by some coaches takes advantage of a small audio-cassette recorder. Here, the coach speaks into a hand-held or throat microphone using a tried and tested system of notation, and events are recorded permanently for subsequent analysis.

All match analysis methods are quantitative in nature and focus basically on either the outcome of a movement (was the attack successful?) or else the frequency with which it occurred (how many times did the player play an unsuccessful backhand volley?). Their application depends on the coach or user clarifying the purpose for which they are used and also the efficiency or 'user-friendliness' of the actual system selected/devised for gathering information. At the end of the day, hard data gained in this manner must be tempered by the coach's own judgement. Brackenridge & Alderson (1985) express this idea which applies to all methods of skill evaluation (p.7):

> The best of all possible worlds, of course, is to combine the knowledge, experience and intuitive judgement of the coach with the accuracy, objectivity and rigour of a good match-analysis system.

Sports skill tests

Match analysis techniques can serve a number of purposes of which the evaluation of skill and provision of feedback is only one. Historically, however the emphasis has been placed on the specific assessment of playing ability in particular sports through the use of purpose-designed skill tests or batteries of tests (for example, Campbell & Tucker, 1967; Mood, 1980). A number of tests have been used to measure the notion of 'motor ability' — supposedly a quality which predisposes those who possess it to success in many sports. Such a notion has fallen into disrepute since the acceptance that skill is, by and large, specific. Tests have also been devised to predict skill in military, industrial and sporting contexts. These too have proved to have very limited success — with perhaps the exception of tests employed by the military to assess flying

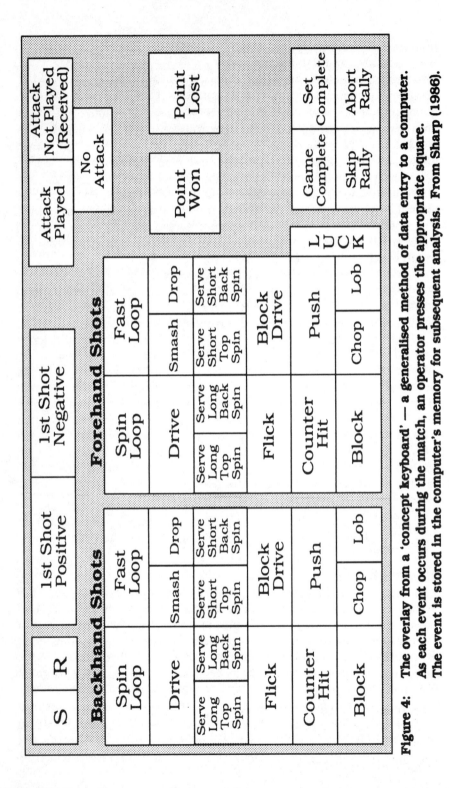

Figure 4: The overlay from a 'concept keyboard' — a generalised method of data entry to a computer. As each event occurs during the match, an operator presses the appropriate square. The event is stored in the computer's memory for subsequent analysis. From Sharp (1986).

personnel — probably because the criteria or abilities required for prediction are not fully understood.

Sports skills tests are rather dated in concept today — most of the effort devoted to devising appropriate batteries of tests to assess say, skill in basketball or handball took place some 30/40 years ago. Although their use in North America is fairly widespread, they serve the British coach or teacher today only as a basis for the design of proficiency award schemes in some sports and for evaluating performance in specific skill situations. In a school setting they have limited application as a means of evaluating the progress of physical education pupils and providing targets to achieve. A brief discussion will illustrate these points.

A typical sports skill battery includes a series of tests each designed to measure performance in a particular component of the game. For example, one particular basketball test includes items such as a front shot, side shot, foul shot, speed pass, jump and reach test, overarm pass for accuracy and dribble test. A battery for field hockey includes tests to measure speed of dribbling, push pass for speed and accuracy, obstacle dribble and goal shot, penalty corner hit and corner hit for speed and accuracy. Some test batteries also include items which would more correctly be labelled as fitness tests.

The items making up tests are selected on the basis of complicated statistical procedures and designed so that they reflect the game in the most accurate way possible. Most test batteries are published with clear instructions and equipment requirements, and sometimes provide the user with normative data for comparing the scores of individuals. The single largest problem with such tests is that they lack validity. They may be high in reliability, but, by and large they do not accurately reflect skill in the game proper. This is because they only include components which are simple to define (e.g., penalty corner hit) and which are relatively easily and objective to assess. They tend to exclude critical elements such as tactical play, decision making ability, anticipation and game aware-ness, which are often the essence of the game.

The value of such tests is limited to instances where the user wishes an approximate measure of sporting skill. They certainly provide motiva-tion and success through the attainment of clear and well defined goals and in this sense they may serve to encourage beginners in a new sport because they do provide tangible aims and realistic goals to achieve. Any user however, must bear in mind whether the test is a valid indicator of overall skill level and also consider whether the time spent testing would be better devoted to purposeful practice. One positive way in which sports skill tests have been used is in the area of proficiency award schemes.

Proficiency award schemes

Proficiency schemes have a long history and are well-established in most sports (e.g., Thistle awards in athletics, Britoil awards in gymnastics and the Star tests in canoeing). Just as sports skills tests are based on performance of selected components, proficiency tests examine technical competence in a range of areas. For example, the Britoil scheme assesses competence in basic rolling and balancing activities. The Scottish Basketball scheme examines skill in a number of activities such as free shooting, repetition passing and dribbling. Most schemes are tiered to suit different age groups and/or sexes and graded to allow progression from easy to more challenging tasks. Assessment may be a combination of visual observation (qualitative assessment) and objective scoring (e.g., time to complete a shuttle run) and is carried out usually by a teacher or youth leader at the lower levels and a more experienced coach at higher levels.

By and large, proficiency schemes have evolved through the interest of governing bodies to encourage participation and the belief that a 'wider base' may produce increased excellence at the top end of the sport. Through the selling of badges, medals, certificates and the like there is also a financial return for governing bodies. As far as the learner is concerned, proficiency awards serve a number of purposes. They provide tangible recognition of achievement and a common yardstick for comparing individuals as well as providing realistic goals for beginners. They also provide the coach with targets and materials to aid his/her own planning. In addition, because award schemes are progressive in their challenge, they are intrinsically motivating and so encourage beginners to remain in sport when there would otherwise be insufficient external reason for them to stay. The expectation is that by the time an individual completes the scheme, he/she has a strong enough intrinsic desire to improve and continue without further artificial reward.

These are very laudable intentions but the extent to which they are achieved hinges on a number of factors. Coaches and others must be given access to such tests; they should cater for divergent groups — different sexes, ages, and possibly people with disabilities; they should provide challenge and interest and therefore be game-related; they should be simple, reliable and quick to administer; and the rewards should encourage learners to work through the scheme.

Formative and summative evaluation

During the course of learning, the coach or teacher is directly concerned with the diagnosis and solution of errors, and also helping the learner develop a greater understanding of skill. The monitoring and assessment which takes place during this period is often referred to as formative assessment. In contrast, measurement of the learner's skill level following an extended period of practice is referred to as summative evaluation. Formative evaluation is concerned with providing information to the learner and focuses on the learning process *per se* whilst summative evaluation aims to summarise the effects of learning. The coach and teacher should be most concerned with formative evaluation; the learner's performance in competition or in a proficiency test serving as a kind of summative evaluation.

Subjective and objective evaluation

These terms have been mentioned many times already. Broadly, all kinds of evaluations are subjective because they are based on human judgement. They differ, however, in the extent to which the individual's own judgement 'colours' the evaluation. Tests which employ sound methodology, clear protocols and efficient measuring instruments are likely to lead to more objective evaluation than those which rely solely on personal impression. Objectivity is critical when there is a need for the coach/teacher to be detached from the learner/performer (as in competition judging or scouting), but is less important at the level of learner/coach. In the latter situation, it may not matter that measurements are exact or that the coach's comments accurately reflect the learner's performance, so long as his performance improves towards the established goals.

Video and skill evaluation

Lyons (1987) has written an excellent text which is devoted entirely to the role of video technology in sport. Lyons describes many different applications of which skill evaluation is only one. A brief summary is presented here in the knowledge that video is used more and more frequently as a tool to evaluate skill.

Video is a very accessible medium. In recent years hardware has reduced in price significantly to the extent that VHS and similar systems can now be purchased by the home user and coach/club alike for a relatively small financial outlay. They can also be hired very cheaply. The fact they are also very portable makes them an ideal medium for capturing sporting action on film. Current designs allow some cameras to be held in the hand of a child. Mainly for these reasons, video has become widely adopted for match analysis in a variety of sports. In some sports it is also used as a tool to provide the learner with performance feedback. For example, many ski instructors have access to portable video cameras which they use on the ski slope to record the actions of novice and expert skiers alike. The inbuilt, camera monitor allows the learner to view him/herself and obtain information almost immediately. In canoeing, one system is available which employs two cameras together with a large monitor and is directed to helping national-level slalomists choose the correct path between gates. The canoeist is filmed paddling down an artificial course. He/she then makes his/her way back, but en route draws into the side to observe his/her actions on a time-delayed monitor. In this way the canoeist can paddle continuously (until fatigued!), attempt gates, receive immediate feedback and then try different lines/techniques to improve performance. In other sports it may not be possible to provide immediate feedback (e.g., during a game of soccer or volleyball) in which case viewing must wait until the game or competition is over.

Video has many, obvious merits. It is highly objective and therefore more acceptable to those who might otherwise doubt what they are told.

It offers the coach a permanent record and allows him/her to observe a learner's performance over and over again and therefore proffer comments which are more likely to be accurate. It allows game details which the coach might not otherwise notice (e.g., actions 'off the ball') to be picked up. It allows actions to be slowed or stopped for detailed analysis. It is also a 'dynamic' means of communication which offers natural appeal to the subject of a recording and it also provides individualised learning.

Balanced against all this however, are some disadvantages. Lyons (1987) lists a variety of which the following are some of the more important. There are practical problems associated with acquisition of hardware, technical awareness and actual use (where to shoot from, when to zoom, etc.). Questions must be asked about whether it really works. This matter was addressed in Chapter 3 and the reader will recall that video only 'works' if certain criteria are adhered to. Video often encourages a very analytical approach which tends to highlight errors at the expense of successes. It should also be noted that video has limited use for quantitative movement analysis (note earlier) because the degree of resolution it offers is usually too poor. And Scully (1988) suggests that video — particularly when used in slow motion mode — may not be very helpful as a demonstration medium. She presents evidence which indicates that whilst slow-motion film helps learners understand the 'relative' motion of body parts (e.g., how the arms move in relation to the trunk), it does not help the learner perceive absolute information concerned with speed and forces. She warns that slow-motion video should be used sparingly in teaching motor skills and this point is highlighted in the comments of Smith (1991: p.15):

> Although video taped examples of dance performance are on the increase, they are poor alternatives to live demonstration. Qualitative details of time, energy and space seem to dissipate or become lost in the flat two-dimensional projected sketch of the original. Moreover, there are many problems in 'taking movement off' a video performance which has to be stopped, started, slowed and rewound manually and is often shown as a front view performance only.

The individual must balance for him/herself the pros and cons. It may be that video is best used with particular sports/activities. What does seem clear though is that, as a tool for skill evaluation, the video camera is potentially a significant aid in helping the coach make accurate and informative decisions about how people perform and learn.

Comparative evaluation

Already in this chapter examples have been given of several ways in which the performance of a player or learner may be examined. This section summarises the essential reasons behind evaluation. To have meaning at all, any kind of measurement has to be referenced against something else. There are three ways this can take place.

Norm-referencing

Norm-referencing takes place when comparisons are made with other people. This approach is typical of competitive situations where one person's skill or the performance of a team is matched against another. Any ranking or league system employs norm-referencing. A squash ladder is a good example. Any one player's performance is indicated by position on the ladder. It doesn't say exactly how good a player is but merely indicates their performance in relation to others in the table. The Olympic games provides another example. The athlete who wins a gold medal is not necessarily the best performer — just the best performer on the day of those who took part in the competition.

Norm-referencing seems to fulfil two purposes: selection and motivation. Selection plays a part in both amateur and professional sport. Members of the United States Olympic squad are selected on a 'first three past the line' principal. Professional soccer teams are promoted or relegated depending on whether they end up in the top or bottom positions of the division. In these and similar situations, selection is a very powerful force. Vast amounts of money, status and career prospects hinge on such decisions. Until recently, assessment in school physical education was based largely on this system. Norm-referenced evaluation provides a strong sense of motivation and competition. Thus when people are evaluated with respect to others they will often compete vigorously to do better.

Norm-referencing clearly has an important part to play, especially in competitive situations, but it has limitations. It means for example that some players will always fail — for some to succeed implies that others must fall by the wayside! This is particularly unfair if those who do fail are still good performers (e.g., the athlete who misses Olympic selection because he/she is injured on selection day, but otherwise holds the best performance that year). In a school context, norm-referencing means that half of all children will always perform less well than the average, despite the strengths and qualities of those in the lower half. And it says nothing about their strengths or weaknesses. Norm-referencing provides no information which a teacher or coach can use in deciding how to take remedial action to improve performance or the effectiveness of teaching/coaching. It is natural, of course, for people — especially sports people — to compare themselves with others. In terms of skill learning however, apart from providing additional motivation (or the opposite) there is little value in norm-referencing. It is the learner who is important and how he/she measures up against him/herself which should be the focus of attention.

Self-referencing

Self-referencing takes place when the learner's performance is compared against a previous performance: it is the normal course of events when a coach or teacher works with an athlete on matters such as technique or fitness. An athlete who monitors weekly resting pulse or keeps a record of personal-best performance over each season is adopting a self-referencing model. Self-referencing is especially meaningful with specific groups of learners. For example, teachers, physiotherapists and coaches who work with people with disabilities are only concerned with the individual's rate of progress. Because of the special nature of some injuries and disabilities, it is meaningless to compare individuals, even if similarly disabled. For similar reasons, the assessment of young and old learners as well as beginners, should focus on the individual and not others.

Criterion-referencing

In contrast to norm-referencing, criterion-referencing sets out to describe exactly what a learner has achieved, and comparisons of one learner's performance with another's are irrelevant. Criterion-referencing measures an individual's performance against previously determined targets or external standards. In competitive sport there are a number of examples. An athlete's performance may be compared with an Olympic qualifying standard or a world record. In these situations, it does not matter how the person fares with regard to others (many others may meet the qualifying standard, or they may not); it is the relation of the athlete's performance to the standard which counts.

Those tests which contain a safety element often use criterion-referencing. One example is a motor car driving test where the examiner is concerned that the candidate reaches a minimum level of mastery to ensure road safety. Another is the life-saving award where assessment has to ensure the individual has the minimum knowledge and skill to save life. In the same way, to gain the coaching awards of many governing bodies, the candidate has to meet criteria relating to knowledge and understanding as well as technical execution.

As far as learning is concerned, it follows that in order to provide the learner with informative and relevant feedback, the coach or teacher must focus on specific criteria. Such criteria must relate specifically to the technique in question (e.g., how should the feet be positioned, where should the ball be struck) but they may also be established externally. For example, a long jump coach might set as a goal a distance of 6.50m to be reached before the end of the season. The attainment of such a goal will be the result of meeting many other interim targets or criteria throughout the training season. Criterion-/self-referencing should be the model adopted by the teacher or coach. It provides the learner with clear targets for which to strive, provides encouragement through the achievement of tangible goals and makes for clear communication between coach and learner. Criteria have to be established however and this will hinge on the coach's expertise and knowledge. Furthermore, criteria have to be selected in the correct order (see Chapter 5) and pitched at the appropriate level (e.g., the criteria for a successful handstand at club level will differ from those at national level). Criterion-referencing also implies an ongoing, formative kind of evaluation as each target is worked towards and achieved.

Finally, it is worth mentioning that the coach's analysis of which criteria are important should take into account the fact that when people learn, not only do technical changes take place, but also intellectual, physical and attitudinal changes. In other words, the technical model and its requirements will alter as the learner becomes more skilled — but so too will the coach's expectations of the learner's acquisition of related knowledge (rules, history of the sport, league organisation, etc.), as well as changes in attitude (punctuality, sporting behaviour, helping others, etc.) and so on.

Evaluation in practice

The role of the sports coach and the physical education teacher is a demanding and responsible one. It is questionable whether the average club coaches/teachers have the time or the access to modern technology which enables them to evaluate learners in the best possible manner. Probably few coaches have immediate access to video cameras; fewer still have the scientific back-up provided by a national coaching centre or university sports science laboratory. It may also be that most people do not have the time to learn how to use high-tech methods or the time available during a coaching session to introduce complex and highly individualised approaches. In the study by Sharp (1988), coaches raised just these issues and time, above all else, was the critical limitation in evaluation. It is notable that the most frequently used method to monitor the skill of athletes was given as subjective observation (see Table 5, overleaf).

This is the one technique of course, which does not require the use of any resources other than the coach's own personal experience. An extension of this approach is for the coach to keep a diary of each athlete and record the kinds of things which an athlete would also keep in a training diary. The list below shows the kinds of items which would fit most sports.

1. Attendance at training sessions, including reasons for lateness/absence.
2. Aims of preparation; reasons for selection; predictions of the athlete's future performances.
3. Facilities and equipment required.
4. Competitions entered plus entry qualifications.
5. Amount of physical training — days, sessions, rest periods, totals proposed for the year.
6. Details of technical preparation, tactical preparation, mental preparation, theoretical concepts the athlete is expected to understand.

Table 5: Results of a survey (Sharp, 1988) of methods used by coaches to monitor skill, fitness and tactical awareness.

METHODS OF EVALUATION	COMPONENT MEASURED		
	SKILL	TACTICAL	FITNESS
Personal Observation	73	68	63
Views of Other People	54	51	41
Written Recordings	52	41	46
Competition Results	51	54	35
Video Recording	42	33	9
Self-Designed Tests	39	16	56
Match Analysis	34	45	15
Examination of Training Diary	20	16	35
Objectives Tests (published)	19	8	27
Audio Recordings	10	7	3

(all figures given in percentages)

A diary such as this would include all details relevant to the preparation of the athlete and certainly include reference to skill development. Permanent records like this help identify the progress made by learners as well as giving direction to future work. It would seem that in practice, coaches tend to adopt a qualitative approach to skill evaluation relying on their own experience, judgement and intuition. They do adopt other methods as seen in the table above, but by and large, the subjective approach — which is very cost effective in terms of time and resources — is the mainstay of their work.

One of the most important practical things which coaches and teachers should do is structure their analysis. Sharp (1989) describes one way in which this can be done by suggesting that analysis should be viewed as three sequential, but related events: observation, analysis and evaluation. Observation is the process of taking in information about the learner's performance. For observation of performance to be effective it should be reliable (repeated viewing; views from various angles; time to absorb the information, etc.), focused (select particular parts of the performance; pre-setting through prior knowledge; etc.) and accurate (aid memory by taking written notes or using a video camera). Analysis is the process of assessing why errors have arisen. The importance of working with people of varying abilities, which helps the coach or teacher develop a repertoire of potential solutions, should be noted here. Analysis is further aided through video and should always focus on the identification of the root causes of problems and not merely the effects of underlying problems. Evaluation is the end stage and is concerned with decision making and response. The coach or teacher may decide for example, to arrange additional practice for the learner, try a new skill, have a rest or change the activity in question. The net result must be positive, informative and motivating. These three stages — observation, analysis, evaluation — normally gel together and happen immediately. It is good practice however, to reflect on the accuracy of these stages from time to time, if only to confirm good practice.

Finally, the coach should evaluate him/herself or seek feedback from other, more experienced coaches. Bunyan (1991: p.6) makes this point in relation to the teaching of canoeing:

> To effectively evaluate their teaching performance instructors must systematically appraise what they have done in a variety of ways. They must learn to be self-critical, analysing their personal attributes such as voice and non-verbal communication, the appropriateness of the material they have presented, the methods employed to deliver it. Without evaluation a deeper understanding of the teaching situation is unlikely and as a result success and enjoyment will not be optimised.

Some governing bodies assess their coaches using video and there is no reason why the coach should not use a written checklist to examine his/her effectiveness. Shedden & Armstrong (1985) present a coaching evaluation chart which contains questions relating to planning and preparation, management and organisation, communication, and coaching technique. This is designed as a self-checklist to be used either by the coach alone or in conjunction with a more experienced observer.

Summary

1. There are a number of reasons for evaluation — to provide learners with feedback, to establish if the coach's goals have been attained, to determine the success of teaching methods, to examine the long-term progress of learners, to provide records of achievement, to assess competitive performance, to determine potential, to establish 'models' of sport.
2. A number of elements can be measured such as technique, timing, accuracy, amount and frequency.

3.   Measurements are the actual values indicating skill level. Tests are the procedures used to obtain scores. Evaluation is the judgement the coach/teacher places on measurements.
4.   Formative evaluation is ongoing and designed to provide feedback. Summative evaluation summarises many performances over a period of time.
5.   Validity refers to whether a test measures what it purports to measure. Reliability refers to the consistency of a measurement. Objectivity refers to whether a test yields the same measurements with different testers. A test is sensitive if it discriminates between people.
6.   Qualitative measurements refer to the direct visual observation of movement and tend to be subjective in nature. Quantitative measurements involve the precise monitoring of specific aspects of a movement, normally using some kind of technical recording device.
7.   Match analysis is the process of recording particular aspects of a game or player — usually in a team game situation. It has a number of values. To provide the coach with comprehensive 'models' of the game. To provide feedback. To scout and to select team members.
8.   Methods of match analysis range from paper and pencil notation to computerised techniques.
9.   Sports skill tests attempt to measure playing ability in sports through testing the individual on a number of specific skills. They tend to lack validity.
10. Proficiency award schemes are popular with learners and serve a number of purposes. For the learner they help motivate, maintain enthusiasm and also provide tangible evidence of achievement.
11. Video technology is used increasingly to monitor the skill of learners. It has a number of merits including objectivity, permanent recording, slow down/freeze facilities, etc.. Amongst the disadvantages are cost, accessibility, technical operation and poor resolution.
12. Learners can be evaluated with reference to themselves (self-referencing), other people (norm-referencing) or external criteria (criterion-referencing).
13. Effective evaluation is often compromised through lack of time, inadequate resources and poor knowledge.
14. Coaches and teachers should recognise that the evaluation process includes not only the learner but also themselves.

Discussion questions

1.   In your sport, what is the major technique used for evaluation?
2.   Are your methods the same as other coaches?
3.   Is evaluation in your sport given a high enough profile? If not, what do you think are the problems?

4. Do you think that high technology (computers, videos, etc.) has a part to play in the evaluation of learners in your sport?
5. Do you ever examine whether your analysis of learners is correct? For example, is your ability to spot faults as good as it could be?
6. Do you encourage learners to examine their own performances? If so, how do you go about it?
7. How useful is it to assess learners with a view to establishing competition amongst others?
8. Are you ever conscious of telling learners what they are doing wrong instead of telling them how to improve?
9. When you make a comment such as "Good" or "Well done", are you aware of the point of reference (e.g., the learner's previous performance, someone else's performance, your own model)?

References

Brackenridge, C.H. and Alderson, G.J.K. (1985) *Match analysis.* Occasional Paper, Leeds: National Coaching Foundation.

Brown, E.W. (1982) Visual evaluation techniques for skill analysis. *Journal of Physical Education, Recreation and Dance,* 21–26, January.

Bunyan, P. (1991) Making the most of our teaching. *Adventure Education,* **8**, 1, 5–6.

Campbell, W.R. and Tucker, N.M. (1967) *An introduction to tests and measurement in physical education.* London: Bell & Sons.

Cooper, J.M., Adrian, M. and Glassow, R.B. (1982) *Kinesiology* (5th Edition). London: C.V. Mosby.

Franks, I.M. and Goodman, D. (1986) A systematic approach to analysing sports performance. *Journal of Sports Sciences,* **4**, 1–11.

Lee, D.N., Lishman, R.J. and Thomson, J.A. (1982) Regulation of gait in long jumping. *Journal of Experimental Psychology: Human Perception and Performance,* **8**, 448–459.

Lyons, K. (1987) Using *video in sport.* Denby Dale: Springfield Press.

Mood, D.P. (1980) Numbers *in motion.* Palo Alto, CA.: Mayfield Publishing.

National Coaching Foundation (1987) *Improving techniques — Level 1 Video.* The National Coaching Foundation, Leeds.

Radford, K.W. (1991) Link observation, feedback and assessment. *Canadian Journal of Health, Physical Education and Recreation,* **57**, 2, 4–9.

Rowntree, D. (1979) *Assessing students: How shall we know them?* London: Harper & Row.

Schleihauf, R.E. (1979) A hydrodynamic analysis of swimming propulsion. In J. Terauds & E.W. Bedingfield (Eds.), *Swimming III,* International Series on Sport Sciences, Vol. 8, Baltimore: University Park Press.

Scully, D.M. (1988) Visual perception of human movement: The use of demonstrations in teaching motor skills. *British Journal of Physical Education (Research Supplement)*, **19**, 6.

Sharp, R.H. (1986) Player analysis by microcomputer. *Coach education: Preparation for a profession.* Proceedings of the VIII Commonwealth and International Conference on Sport, Physical Education, Dance, Recreation and Health. London: E. & F.N. Spon.

Sharp, R.H. (1988) How do coaches monitor their player? *Scottish Sports Coach*, Jan.

Sharp, R.H. (1989) *Analysis of performance.* Leeds: The National Coaching Foundation.

Shedden, J. and Armstrong, M. (1985) *Effective coaching.* Level 2 Resource Pack. Leeds: National Coaching Foundation.

Smith, J. (1991) Teaching dance performance in secondary education. *British Journal of Physical Education*, **22**, 4, 14–17.

Stewart, J. and Atha, J. (1988) Postural precision in archery. In *Proceedings of the Annual Conference of the British Association of Sports Sciences*, Exeter, September.

Vanderbeck, E. (1979) It isn't right but I don't know what's wrong with it. *Swimming Times*, **16**, 3, 82–84.

Watkins, J. (1983) *An introduction to mechanics of human movement.* London: M.T.P. Press.

Watkins, J. (1987) Qualitative movement analysis. *British Journal of Physical Education*, **18**, 4, 177–179.

Watkins, J. (1987) Quantitative movement analysis. *British Journal of Physical Education*, **18**, 6, 271–275.

Index